Against All Odds

Against All Odds

God at work in an impossible situation

Elizabeth Goldsmith

LONDON ● COLORADO SPRINGS ● HYDERABAD

First published 2007 by Authentic Media and OMF International
9 Holdom Avenue, Bletchley, Milton Keynes, MK1 1QR, UK
1820 Jet Stream Drive, Colorado Springs, CO 80921, USA
Medchal Road, Jeedimetla Village,
Secunderabad 500 055, A.P., India
www.authenticmedia.co.uk
Authentic Media is a division of IBS-STL UK, a company limited by
guarantee (registered charity no. 270162)

OMF International, Station Approach, Borough Green, Kent,
TN15 8BG. www.omf.org.uk

British Library Cataloguing in Publication Data

A catalogue record for this book is available from the British
Library

ISBN-13: 978-1-85078-759-4

Cover Design by fourninezero design.
Print Management by Adare
Printed in Great Britain by J.F. Print, Sparkford

Dedication

To all the dynamic and gifted Malaysian Christians and OMF workers who have shared their lives and memories with me. They represent a multitude of others who laboured to build the large and expanding church in Malaysia today. I have had to be selective in choosing stories for this book, but the grand total of their names is surely written in a better book than this (Rev. 3:5).

Contents

WEST MALAYSIA

0   20   40   60   80
MILES

SOUTH
THAILAND

SONGKHLA
HAADYAI
PATTANI
SADURI
YALA
NARATHIWAT
TANJONG MAT
KOTA BHARU

KEDAH
SUNGEI GOLOK
ALOR SETAR

GEORGETOWN
PENANG PROVINCE
WELLESLEY
SELAMA
PARIT BUNTAR

PERAK
IPOH

KELANTAN   TRENGGANU

TANAH RATA
RINGLET
KUALA LIPIS
KAMPAR
CHENDERIANG
BIDOR   SUNGEI JAN

M A L A Y A

TELUK ANSON
SLIM RIVER
TANJONG MALIM
SUNGEI
MUAR   JERANTUT
BUKIT KOMAN

PAHANG
KUANTAN
GAMBANG

KUALA KUBU
RAWANG
SELANGOR   KARAK   TEMERLOH
BATU ARANG   TRIANG
SUNGEI WAY
KUALA LUMPUR
PENGKALAN   SERDANG

NEGRI
TANJONG SEPAT   SEMBILAN

ALOR   MACHAP GEMAS BAHAU
GELANG   BULOH KASAP   BEKOK
MALACCA   CHAAH
BURIT LIPUT   KALUANG
SUNGI   JAHOR   RENGAM
UJONG   SIMPANG RENGAN
SCUDAI

SINGAPORE

STRAITS

OF

MALACCA

SUMATRA

SOUTH

CHINA

SEA

Introduction

'God has totally failed our family. We went out with such high hopes, but they're shattered now. God doesn't keep his promises. He's let us down. How can I possibly trust him anymore?'

The words came tumbling out of the young father. He gazed at us, the pain and bewilderment etched clearly on his face.

He continued pouring out his story. Everything had gone fine when they began their missionary work. They had found an apartment close to the language school. Local people had been friendly. Their health was good and the climate enjoyable.

Then suddenly everything went wrong. They were forced to move as the landlord wanted the premises, but it was difficult to find anywhere else that was convenient and affordable. So they had to travel a long way each day. The language proved far more complicated than they had expected. And it was frustrating not being able to communicate even simple needs like when their fridge broke down. Their new neighbours were suspicious of them and no one was willing to help. To crown it all, his wife fell seriously ill. They couldn't find a doctor to treat her, and the local hospital proved abysmally inadequate.

We listened to his tale of woe and our hearts went out to him as he struggled to make sense of what had happened.

'Have you ever read how Paul described his own missionary experience?' my husband Martin asked gently. 'God never promised Christian ministry would be a bed of roses. Suffering is a normal part of the Christian life and we shouldn't be surprised at it. We are called to persevere, even when the going's tough. See what Paul wrote . . .' He opened his Bible to 2 Corinthians 4:7–9

> We have this treasure in jars of clay to show that this all-surpassing power is from God and not from us. We are hard pressed on every side, but not crushed; perplexed, but not in despair; persecuted, but not abandoned; struck down, but not destroyed.

'I've never heard *that* preached on,' our friend marvelled. 'In my church we never talk about suffering. We're expecting God to *bless* us. Shouldn't life be wonderful for a Christian? We're serving a great God, and he's supposed to answer our prayers.'

'Yes, but we're also following a Saviour who knew all about persevering through suffering. He tramped the stony paths of Israel because he had no donkey to ride. He was forced to sleep under the stars when no one offered him shelter. And he set his face to go up to Jerusalem even when he knew he would be rejected by many, ridiculed and mocked, and finally cruelly scourged and led out to die the most horrible death.

'He told us, "the servant is not above his master". If you come up against difficulties, it doesn't mean that God has let you down, or that he doesn't love you. We're in a battle. All the forces of evil are working to prevent God's kingdom spreading in this world. If Christ faced so much opposition, how can we be surprised by problems and difficulties when we attempt to follow in his footsteps? Suffering shouldn't deflect us from our mission.'

We spent a long time praying and talking with this young father, as God began to shed a new light on his experiences. Thankfully, with this deeper understanding, he felt able to contemplate returning to his calling with a new trust in God and a determination to follow him regardless of the cost.

He is not the only person we have met who unconsciously pictures God like the genie in Aladdin's lamp. Rub the lamp the right way (pray about it) and God will be there to fulfil our wishes.

But God is not *our* servant, we are *his* servants. And he has the right to order our situation as he sees fit. In this fallen world there will be problems, perplexities and difficulties. We won't always understand why things happen to us. Our calling is to trust, and to persevere with the task given us, in spite of all the problems.

The Apostle Peter tells us that as Christians we are not to be surprised by painful trials and suffering (1 Pet. 4:12). Suffering is not something 'strange'; it is not unexpected in the Christian life. In fact, Peter goes on to say that we are to rejoice when we suffer, because in that suffering we are sharing the sufferings of Christ. Suffering draws us closer to our Lord, as we understand more deeply what he went through. And as we share his heart of suffering love, we begin to see more vividly how deeply God suffers even now as he bears with patience the wilfulness and rebellion of our world. His heart must be continually grieved as he sees all the violence and greed spilling out in every act of sinfulness. Genesis

6:5, 6 tell us that when 'the LORD saw how great man's wickedness . . . had become . . . the LORD was grieved . . . and his heart was filled with pain.' If we have never suffered, how can we begin to understand the depth of pain which God carries even today?

Experiencing suffering can actually enrich us. Paul writes that 'suffering produces perseverance' (Rom. 5:3). This is a quality sadly missing in many of our churches today, where we often look for instant results. The word goes round, 'Try this new method for evangelism.' Or, 'This is the sure way to produce instant church growth.' And we all jump onto the bandwagon – until it becomes evident that this particular gimmick was not the quick solution for which we had hoped. But God's way of working in nature is slow and quiet and often imperceptible. We need steady perseverance to continue in faithfulness even when the apparent results are small.

And 'perseverance produces character', or a personality which has been tried and tested and so develops sterling qualities. There is no short cut for this. Like an athlete's persistent training, week after week and month after month, so a rich Christian character can only develop as it is stretched and tested. And 'character produces hope', or that strong confidence in God which comes when we have proved his faithfulness again and again in times of trouble.

Background

This book is about a team of Christian workers who faced many difficulties in order to bring the gospel to West Malaysia, but who pressed on nevertheless. At first the work of spreading the gospel depended considerably on overseas missionaries, but soon local Christians began to play a major part in building the present dynamic and strong Malaysian church. Indeed it was the national Christians who revolutionized the whole situation, taking the lead in every area of church life. They brought much-needed dynamic growth.

Consequently I not only want to tell the exciting stories of some early missionary pioneers, but also of God's amazing work in the lives of key national believers. I owe a debt to Yap Heong Mong, the warm-hearted Director of OMF in Malaysia. She arranged a detailed itinerary for me to meet many Malaysian Christians who were influenced in their early life by OMF. Their stories thrilled my heart, since my husband Martin and I had worked as missionaries in this country during the 1960s.

This book opens in the early 1950s. The Overseas Missionary Fellowship of the China Inland Mission had just come through the trauma of rejection and hostility where they had been working in China. The political situation had intensified until even their closest friends began to beg them to leave. The Communist government, which had ordered their departure, was also spreading anti-Christian Marxism throughout South East Asia. No one knew if the neighbouring countries would succumb to the new ideology. Some feared that Malaya, whose name changed to West Malaysia with independence in 1957, might be next and the missionaries would have only a few years before being thrown out again.

But they grasped the opportunity to bring the gospel to Malaya, making the most of the challenging situation. As their time of opportunity lengthened, they persevered against the odds, steadily evangelizing and teaching, with no idea of the amazing results that God would later give. It probably never occurred to them that within 20 years the growth of the local church would render them superfluous.

In many parts of the world today where opposition to the Christian faith is increasing, this message of perseverance needs to be heard. In Europe, materialistic secularism and post-modern pluralism appear to have won the day. Upholding Christian standards on homosexual practice and abortion may in the future lead to imprisonment. Witness in a school or workplace may incur active hostility where the post-modern supermarket mentality espouses 'tolerance' as the essential attribute. Yet the same people who advocate tolerance remain strongly intolerant towards those with faith in an absolute truth.

Christians witnessing in many countries encounter constant harassment and official opposition. Some countries forbid the preaching of the gospel and even imprison Christ's followers. Some severely persecute those who turn from the predominant or official religion of that country. More and more followers of Christ are being required to sacrifice even life itself for his sake.

Faced with the present challenging situation, what are we who know and honour our Lord Jesus going to do about it? The story of the Overseas Missionary Fellowship's work in Malaysia can bring us new confidence that God is not dismayed by problems. He is not discouraged when the odds pile against us.

Up and down Malaysia today God is answering prayer. Many Chinese and Indians are becoming Christians. New church buildings are bursting at the seams, with dedicated and visionary leaders. And from Malaysia the gospel is spreading to the surrounding nations. How has this come about when only 50 years ago there were so few Christians and witness for Christ was so difficult? That is the question this book seeks to answer. The map at the beginning of the book and the glossary of Chinese names at the end should help readers follow the events described.

Every Christian has been given a commission to spread the good news of Jesus Christ throughout the world. Let us all take up the fresh challenges of today, believing God's promise from Galatians 6:9:

> Don't get tired of doing what is good. Don't get discouraged and give up, for we will reap a harvest of blessing at the appropriate time. (*Living Water*)

1.

The Daunting Challenge

Guerrillas and political upheaval

The front-page headlines of the *Straits Times*, Malaya's English language daily, screamed: 'Terrorists ambush bus and set it on fire. Passengers stranded on jungle road as darkness fell.' 'European planter shot dead near his home on a rubber estate.'

The traumatic news continued, 'The country is coming under increasing pressure from Communist guerrillas. They creep out of their hiding places in the jungle to derail trains, burn buses, overturn lorries, and disrupt life, causing widespread suffering and bloodshed. Rubber trees are slashed with knives and precious latex lost, striking a severe blow at the economy of the country.'[1] This was Malaya in 1948.

Communism had gained power throughout the length and breadth of Malaya's giant neighbour, China, and its influence was now spreading to outlying countries where substantial groups of Chinese lived and traded. The terrible onslaughts of the Japanese armies in the Federated States of Malaya had been overcome a mere three years earlier. Now a rising tide of Communist guerrilla activity faced the British Mandate. Britain had been desperately impoverished by the superhuman efforts which had been required of her during the Second World War. She felt she badly needed the income from Malaya's rubber and tin in order to rebuild her nation. Forced to take action against the Communists, a State of Emergency was declared in that same year.

But Malaya provided ideal cover for guerrilla activity. A long narrow belt of fertile rice fields, rubber estates and tin mines, about 50 miles wide, stretched up the west coast. On the east coast were a few small fishing villages and towns. But the main sweep of the country, including the central chain of mountains, was covered by dense tropical jungle. Here the guerrillas could conceal their camps and weapons, emerging at will to attack government forces or to raid the scattered hamlets for food and other provisions.

Within a year, a thousand British soldiers and local police had been killed in the fighting. Then Sir Henry Guerney, the British High Commissioner, was assassinated on a jungle road in 1951.

General Sir Gerald Templar, who was appointed to take command, realized that drastic action was needed if the British were to gain the upper hand. So he gave the order: all Chinese not living in a town must be gathered into resettlement areas. Barbed wire would surround the camps, strict curfew would be imposed, and exit and entry would be allowed only through well-guarded gates where everyone would be searched for weapons or food which might be passed to the insurgents. Some six hundred New Villages were eventually set up with nearly three-quarters of a million people living in them. Most of these towns were carved out of the jungle. Others were established on land which was already worked for tin and therefore sterile, with the underground drainage spoiled by the movement of ground.

'It's all commotion in the Malayan forests!' Leslie Lyall,[2] a China Inland Mission (CIM) leader, wrote in his report on the situation. 'The Chinese are on the move – and in a hurry. The homes where they have lived as rubber-tappers or farmers or tin miners are being pulled down and moved on trucks or bicycles or just strong shoulders into New Villages.'

'The government orders are stern!' Nora Rowe exclaimed as she watched it all happening.[3] 'Everything must be taken or destroyed, and nothing left behind that could give shelter or be useful to terrorists. Several days are needed to pull down the usable parts of the old house and erect it in the allotted space in the New Village. But the Chinese never like change, and there is often great reluctance to leave the familiar, even though it was insecure, and go into the camp.'

Leslie Lyall continued,

> Families accustomed to living alone, scattered about in inaccessible jungle valleys, are being brought together to commence a community life, new and strange to them. . . .
>
> The atmosphere and appearance of the resettlement areas must be akin in some respect to the boomtowns of pioneer days in the American West. New houses, new shops, new schools spring up over night. While the enemy lurking in the surrounding forest puts everyone on their guard, and officials move around very cautiously.

But barbed wire is no barrier to ideas.

Would concentrating all these people in the New Villages be enough to foil the strategies of the Communists? The British Mandate soon had to admit that, on its own, resettlement could not achieve their goal. But was there a viable alternative?

In God's amazing grace, Leslie Keeble and Gordon Ward, two former CIM missionaries, were working for General Templar as resettlement officers.[4] They spoke up, 'Christianity is the only answer to Communism. Only Christ can change people's hearts.' General Templar had watched their work and regarded these two men very highly. So the general invited the Overseas Missionary Fellowship of the CIM, alongside some other missions, to send personnel to live in the New Villages and proclaim the life-changing gospel of Christ. He also called for a hundred Christian nurses who could give medical aid throughout the area.

To respond would present a huge challenge for the mission; but the British authorities hoped that this new plan would be an effective means of countering Communist propaganda. Although the general's motives were probably largely political, God used these circumstances to open the door for evangelism.

In God's amazing timing, 1948 had been a peak year for the CIM in China. Recovering quickly after the trauma of war, over 770 CIM missionaries were active in China. But within a short time after the Communist rise to power in 1949 they were all forced to leave and faced some searching questions. What should they do? Had God finished with the CIM? They had been called to mission in the farthest reaches of China. Should they now disband, as their task was no longer possible? Or should they find openings elsewhere? And, if the latter, where could they most effectively use their gifts and the experience they had already gained?

This was the dilemma facing the CIM leadership as they gathered in Bournemouth in 1951 to fast and pray and seek God's leading. Among the rank and file of missionaries, opinions were sharply divided as to whether or not to continue as a mission. It was painful to feel such disunity and difficult at first to be sure of what God was saying into the situation. But as they considered the many millions of Chinese people scattered in other Asian countries, General Templar's request came as an additional confirmation that they should not disband but refocus on the Chinese diaspora wherever they might be found. So, in faith, a call was issued to relocate to other Asian countries and to face the new challenges of the post-war situation.

The new situation would be far from easy. Could the outcast CIM rally its forces once more? Were they prepared to begin at the bottom again, living in primitive conditions, facing unaccustomed tropical heat, adapting to new cultures and learning dialects and languages? Were there still volunteers of the same calibre as the early CIM missionaries who, nearly a hundred years earlier, had faced the vast unknown land of China? With the Communist threat to Malaya being so strong, it was uncertain how long even that door might remain open. 'I was advised to take only a Bible and a small suitcase with me,' one missionary recalled. 'The emergency situation was said to be so uncertain no one knew if we could last even a couple of years.'

Having completed his strategic exploratory trip, Leslie Lyall highlighted the unique opportunity that Malaya presented at that time.

> Here is where the Christian Church faces one of the greatest challenges in the world today. . . a large section of the Chinese population of Malaya, hitherto inaccessible to the gospel messenger, is now brought together near the main highways in settlements where the administrative authorities are *begging* – *yes, begging* – the

missionary to come and work. . . . It will be a tragedy if the Christian Church fails to meet the need now. For the consequence will be that other creeds will eventually gain a firmer hold than ever. The need is of the utmost urgency and calls for *positive action now.*

But what a challenge the missionaries would face. Leslie's article continued,

Missionary work conducted from the security and comfort of an old-established town will not meet this need. Only *residence* in the New Villages can do this. It will mean living with the people under the same kind of thatched roof as theirs; sharing the labours and difficulties of building up a new town and community; teaching in the school, perhaps, or giving practical help with their farms and livestock . . . organising the young people in healthy and character-building occupations; setting a high standard of industry and cheerfulness; and above all presenting and representing the saving gospel of Jesus Christ by every means at our disposal.

Historical context

Research revealed that Christian missionaries had reached the Malayan peninsula some centuries earlier, but the number of Christians was still pitifully small. The capture of Malacca by the Portuguese in 1511 had done little to recommend the Prince of Peace to the local Malays, although the Jesuits laid the foundations for the development of the Roman Catholic Church. Dutch rule from 1640 to 1795 gave the opportunity for Protestant Christianity to be proclaimed. With strategic foresight, the Dutch translated the New Testament into Malay in

1668 – the very first translation of the New Testament into an Asian language. It was used as the main textbook in schools and resulted in a few small Malay-language churches.

In neighbouring Indonesia, churches planted by the Dutch at this time began to take root and grow throughout the following centuries among the indigenous people. But sadly, the British, who fought to win control of the Malay States, refused to allow evangelism of the indigenous Malay population. They feared strong Muslim reaction, which would make governing the country difficult. British colonialism was more focused on trade and economics than spiritual issues. This has left a shackling legacy right down to today. And, alas, many missionaries allowed themselves to be bound by the same chains, passing on their fears and inhibitions to their new converts.

Robert Morrison of the London Missionary Society, who arrived in Canton in 1807, was the first Protestant missionary who worked in that vast land. It was not until 1815 that William Milne, Robert Morrison's colleague, settled in Malacca and Protestant witness began to move forward. Dr Gutzlaff (sometimes called the grandfather of the CIM), the austere Miss Aldersey and Samuel Dyer (whose daughter married Hudson Taylor), also worked in Malaya in the 1820s and 1830s. But when China became accessible, the centre of missionary interest shifted to that vast population[5] and few were left to carry on Christian witness in Malaya.

One hundred years later, that process was to be reversed as missionaries from China moved to Malaysia. God had not forgotten the peoples of Malaya.

By 1948, when the emergency began, there were only about twenty thousand church members in Malaya,[6] out of a total population of 5,849,000 (comprised of Malays and the smaller Indian and Eurasian communities as well as about 2,615,000 Chinese).[7] Their churches had largely been established by Presbyterian, Methodist, Anglican and Brethren missionaries working in the major towns. Dr John Sung's amazingly fruitful evangelistic tours, as he spoke in the power of God to overflowing audiences of overseas Chinese in the 1930s, had added considerably to their number. A Chinese scholar who had studied in the United States, Dr Sung had given up a brilliant career in order to devote himself to evangelism. Wherever he went throughout South East Asia revival broke out. Many church leaders who we met in the 1960s owed their conversion to him.

There were also groups of Christians among immigrants from the south-eastern provinces of the Chinese mainland, as considerable church growth had taken place in these provinces. Five hundred people from Foochow settled near Yong Peng in Johor and brought with them the Chinese Episcopal Church, while Methodists came to found a stronghold around Sitiawan in Perak. Immigrant Chinese Presbyterians also settled in Johor and Anglicans in Singapore.[8] So churches using several of the local Chinese dialects were formed in some main towns.

But apparently some of the established denominational churches were hesitant to welcome a new mission coming into their midst.[9] Hastening to assure them that they were not out to sheep-steal, the OMF leaders stressed that they wanted to support the existing churches, working with anyone who had a Bible-based ministry. It was also obvious that the older churches had insufficient personnel to cover all the New Villages which were being established.[10] Once thus reassured, existing churches were grateful that there were people willing to face the challenge of the tough life in the resettlement camps.

Working closely with the recently established New Villages Co-ordinating Committee and the older Malayan Christian Council, OMF began to place their workers.

Many difficulties faced the new teams arriving in Malaya, and they needed great perseverance to overcome them. The future rich harvest, which we can see today, was still concealed from their view.

Persevering despite danger

Life in the Federation of Malaya during the Emergency could be very dangerous. One missionary recalls:[11]

> For one of the early survey trips I was given the use of an old Morris car. I was driving alone past a notoriously dangerous area through dense rubber trees. All cars were travelling at maximum speed. The purpose was to get through as quickly as one could without ambush or attack. Suddenly, in the middle of this stretch of road my car broke down. Try as I could, I was unable to repair it or find out what was wrong. In desperation I tried to flag down cars and lorry drivers for help, but all my requests were grimly ignored. At last a lorry driver was willing to stop. Leaving his engine running for a fast get-away, he made the repairs.
>
> Waiting for deliverance that day, I had never felt so lonely in all my life.
>
> On another occasion my wife and I were returning from a meeting. It was late and very dark. Suddenly I heard a shot and a bullet hit the upright on the passenger side between the front and back window. Wonderfully it did not penetrate the metal work.
>
> 'I do wish you wouldn't drive so fast,' my wife complained, 'that stone could have smashed our windscreen.' I assured her it was nothing we had hit on the road. When

we reached home I showed her how very near she had been to having a bullet through her head.[12] The deep indentation caused by the bullet in the metalwork showed clearly right next to her face!

A new worker[13] driving with his wife and two children in his little roofless baby Austin met another type of danger. One day, as he was climbing a long, steep hill, a black panther suddenly stepped out onto the road ahead and began trotting up the hill in front of them.

'I thought that maybe I'd better not try to pass it,' he later commented wryly.[14]

Don Fleming, a coal mining chemical engineer, was among the first group of new OMF workers to sail from England for Malaya. He arrived in Singapore in October 1952 and, as there was no orientation or language school, he left after two days for Kuala Lumpur. We have his vivid first impressions in writing.[15]

> Since Malaya was in the throes of the Emergency, the train I left by was preceded by a single engine, travelling backwards and pushing an extra tender in front of it. The idea was that the first tender would blow up any bombs placed on the track by terrorists through the night, and that the train with all its passengers . . . would be warned and stop in time!
>
> The fuel for the engines was old rubber tree logs, sawn up into suitable lengths . . .
>
> We stopped at all the stations, or in between them if anyone wanted to board the train and did not want to walk to the station in the sun. The Malay gentlemen would simply walk out to the track from their atap houses, hold up their hands when the train appeared, and then when it stopped, with their wives and children they would clamber on board.

The Emergency presented a constant danger to all who ventured outside a New Village's barbed-wire perimeter fence. All of the European planters armed themselves with guns, which they kept by them day and night. Even their wives learned how to shoot. And often outside the police stations a silent form would be lying on a stretcher, covered by a white sheet – the body of some Communist who had been brought in for identification.[16]

But missionaries and guns don't belong together. They must put their trust in constant prayer to their heavenly Father and carry on regardless.

Snakes and scorpions found throughout this jungle-covered land, not infrequent but unwelcome visitors to houses, posed a different sort of danger. The workers told many tales of snakes in those early days. Ann Walker in Buloh Kasap, Johor, photographed a huge ten-foot python which had been found asleep with a full stomach in her neighbour's chicken run. When someone attempted to kill it, the snake vomited out the fowl and tried to slither tail-first out through the wire netting. Fortunately it didn't get away.

During my own time there, I was once called to see a snake that someone had killed. They had severed the head from the body and thought it must be dead. But, as we entered the room, its mouth opened wide and it spat its poison towards us! Crushing its head to finish it off, my friend and I thought of the promise that the coming Messiah would 'crush the serpent's head' (Gen. 3:15) – only thus could he be finally defeated.

The new volunteers who were offering themselves for service had to face all of these dangers. But they had read our Lord's call to his disciples as he sent them out in mission: 'anyone who does not take up his cross and follow me is not worthy of me. Whoever finds his life will lose it, and whoever loses his life for my sake will

find it' (Mt. 10: 38, 39). They responded wholeheartedly
and were not afraid of suffering because they knew that
it was the necessary precondition for new life to come to
Malaya.

Persevering despite hostility

'The British Government has uprooted us from our own
homes, and now they are sending spies to actually live
among us. What right have these westerners to live next
door? What ulterior motive do they have for being
here?'

These were some of the accusations flying around the
New Villages as the missionaries tried to settle in.
Children and young people were frequently warned
against them, told to keep away and not listen to their
stories. In one New Village a grandmother observed
every visitor to the missionaries' house and spoke to
each one as they left, warning them against the foreigners. Another woman incited boys to tear down the
gospel posters on the outside walls. Rusty tacks bore
mute witness to the effectiveness of the opposition.[17]

Almost ten years later my husband Martin visited the
New Village of Rasa as a young missionary, nicknamed
Little Moscow because it was so strongly Communist.
He still remembers the hostile stares and atmosphere of
animosity which permeated that place. Perseverance in
the face of enmity and hatred is not easy. Consistent,
patient love was the only answer. And this quality of
love only comes when the Holy Spirit himself pours it
into our hearts.

Persevering against idolatry

'Each house has its idol shrine outside,' wrote Nora Rowe in the early 1950s.[18] 'Dutiful small boys climb up on stools and put in another stick of incense, bowing solemnly three times to each idol. Candles burn outside the houses on the first and fifteenth of each lunar month. And food is placed outside on plates for the use of the spirits of the ancestors in another world.'

Then she added, 'with militant Communism on the one side and darkest heathenism on the other, in the midst of a good deal of material prosperity, how these people need to know Him who said, "My glory I will not give to another".'

Special festivals heralded lavish displays of idolatry.

> Late one evening a crowd of musicians made melody at the door of the temple, its frontage no wider than a shop. Giant candles blazed within, and upon huge trestle tables there was piled before the gaudy idols a truly stupendous quantity of food, ranging from an entire roast pig to bottles of beer and four-foot pyramids of cakes, enough to satiate several hundred people. The Chinese of Malaya are ardent Buddhists, not instructed or philosophical Buddhists, perhaps, but in practice wedded to idolatry both in home and shrine.[19]

Yet one often found a strange mixture of old and new in these New Villages. An article in OMF's magazine *The Millions* vividly describes a funeral.[20]

> All night the priests have been chanting, beating gongs and prostrating themselves before the pictured Goddess of Mercy. Money has been thrown into the river to buy water from the spirit of the river to wash the face of the

dead. Fronds of bamboo, paper streamers and incense all play their part in this funeral. The whole atmosphere is heavy with idolatry as the coffin is brought out. The hired band comes last, but the air it plays sounds strangely familiar. Can it be? Yes, it is the old hymn, 'Nearer my God to Thee, nearer to Thee'!

Letter after letter home told of the struggle against the forces of darkness permeating the atmosphere and their powerful stranglehold. It was clearly evident that 'the god of this age has blinded the minds of unbelievers, so that they cannot see the light of the gospel of the glory of Christ, who is the image of God' (2 Cor. 4:4). Only prayer to God himself could dispel the darkness of unbelief. So the missionaries called out to their prayer partners to stand with them in the work, believing that 'the weapons we fight with . . . have divine power to demolish strongholds' (2 Cor. 10:4). They clung to the hope that, through persistent prayer, even in the hardest places people can be drawn into the kingdom of God.

Persevering despite difficult living conditions

Life in the New Villages presented many unexpected hazards. 'We drove along a row of New Village houses, one just like the next, and stopped to visit one of the OMF stations,' a visiting mission leader commented.

A young couple with their six-month-old baby lived there. The concrete floor looked hard, but it had not been hard enough to keep out a thief who, in traditional Chinese style, had dug underneath the front door and wriggled into the room . . . helping himself to their possessions. No ceiling separated the living room from the metal roof. The iron sheeting collected heat from the tropical sun and beamed it toward the concrete floor. That couple lives in a constant bath of perspiration.

As we drove along the street of the next New Village . . . a lone lady missionary greeted us; her fellow worker was away at the time. It is an anti-Christian, pro-Communist village. One day the morning search of rubber-tappers revealed a matchbox abnormally heavy. Opened, it was found to contain rice. The tappers were all searched again. Unusually, every one of them was found to be carrying matchboxes. When the boxes were opened, it was discovered that each one was packed with uncooked rice, which they were smuggling to the guerrillas.

In these pro-Communist villages, fear of reprisals from the terrorists often kept people away from visiting the missionaries.

Ralph Toliver continued his article:

The typical object of a New Village . . . is the high double barbed wire fence, called the perimeter. By day, the British army controls the roads and seeks to control the countryside. But by night, anyone or anything outside the barbed wire is fair game for the Communist guerrillas. Some villages have the privilege of electricity; then all perimeter fences are ablaze with lights, giving the impression of a well-lit street encircling the village.

The tin mines in the north scatter white and yellow blotches on the green landscape, the desolate dump-heaps jarring the eye. Many of the mines work twenty-four hours a day, which means that some of the men must return home after dark. The Communists recently caught a crew on their way home at three o'clock in the morning, appropriated their lamps, and then walked –

as the tin miners – through the gate in the barbed wire
which was opened for them. They killed the local
guards, stole their guns and ammunition, and escaped
into the jungle.

One sees the Europeans . . . in the towns, holster on
hip, or careering at breakneck speed down the highways
in makeshift armoured cars. Shades of the tin-tailings are
reflected in ashen faces, drawn with inner tension; each
is absorbed in the task of outliving this war with the Red
terrorists. Strain too is written on the face of a missionary here and there, not from fear but from the mere fact
of living [here] . . . as an unwelcome guest.[21]

A New Zealand nurse who joined two other missionaries
in Bekok New Village described her life in an atap-roofed
house. The overlapping fronds of the atap palm made it
cooler than corrugated iron, but it necessitated a peculiar
early-morning routine. When she woke up she would have
to stand up on her camp bed and shake off all the creepy-
crawlies and other debris which had fallen onto her mos-
quito net during the night. Then she would untuck the net
and poke her head out to carefully examine the floor,
making sure there were no snakes or scorpions nearby. The
floor was mud, baked hard, though some missionaries
attempted to seal it with wax. Coarse brown paper served
as wallpaper, covering the cracks in their wooden walls. To
brighten up the room, gospel posters were hung on either
side of the front door and Bible pictures placed where the
idol shelf of the previous owners had stood. Kerosene
lamps were lit each evening, as they had no electricity.

But there was one great advantage of the house: they
were not charged any rent as no one else would live
there because the previous owner had been murdered.

Regardless of the difficulties, they stuck to their task
and learned to adapt, overcoming in God's strength and

tenaciously clinging to the hope that one day they would see a harvest.

Persevering despite the climate

The tropical climate proved a formidable enemy to the western missionaries. Most of them came from more temperate climates, where winters brought invigorating ice and snow, and summer temperatures would not usually rise above 28°C. The perpetual heat of 30° to 40°C, in addition to 95 per cent humidity, proved very draining.

I remember the frustration of trying to write an air-mail letter home in my first week in the tropics, as the perspiration from my hand ruined the letter with its blotches. Even to dry myself after a shower made me perspire. The only thing to do was to laugh it off and to 'drip dry' as we called it. But energy was sapped and I felt constantly below par. Air conditioning was not yet available, and in the New Villages when electricity was available it was so unreliable that even fans generally failed to rotate the sultry air. I had great difficulty struggling to my feet after an afternoon siesta and going in a daze to face the language teacher.

Those used to variety in foliage and colour also found the lack of different seasons monotonous. Calendars from home with refreshing views of winter snows and spring flowers helped to compensate a little here.

The climate also brought exposure to tropical diseases. In those days cholera and typhoid were still rife, and even smallpox reared its ugly head from time to time. Fortunately there were inoculations against these three. But dysentery could be easily contracted in the unhygienic conditions. This sapped one's strength and, if not treated effectively, could be fatal for babies. Children frequently picked up parasitic worms in their play and often these were not discovered for some time. Happily there were not many malaria-carrying mosquitoes, but others carried dengue fever, a debilitating disease against which there was no prophylactic.

I remember once meeting Martin at the airport when he was desperately ill with dengue fever. His high temperature had burnt up his body tissue so drastically that his shirt looked as if it were hanging on a coat hanger instead of his shoulders. Even after he had recovered, he ached deep in his bones for months afterwards.

Keeping cheerful and optimistic in such conditions was not easy.

Persevering despite language difficulties

Perhaps one of the most challenging difficulties was the myriad of local, mutually unintelligible, dialects spoken by the Chinese to whom the missionaries had been sent. Those who had worked in China found that the more educated could understand Mandarin, but it soon became obvious that the different dialects were the heart-languages of the people and must be mastered.

There were carefully-designed courses, with efficient grammar books and dictionaries, for learning Mandarin. But for the other Chinese languages there were few written aids. Each missionary had to find a language helper. But these helpers were not trained in linguistic skills and often could not explain the rules governing the system of tones and the structures of the language. They also found it difficult to explain Chinese idioms and how to express oneself in a more genuinely Chinese way.

Even after two and a half years of language study, for instance, Betty Meadows found that holding a conversation in Cantonese was still beyond her. 'Lord, help me to understand Cantonese,' she pleaded, 'otherwise . . .' The fear she had never voiced was welling up, refusing to be suppressed any longer. '*Otherwise I shall have to go home!*'[22]

To her despairing cry the Lord provided an unexpected and, for her, frustrating answer. She was moved to Mambang Di-Awan where she shared a dark, gloomy wooden shop-front house with a missionary nurse who was often away. A Chinese woman carrying a baby, with a toddler staggering beside her and two older children trailing along, entered the house and began speaking non-stop to her.

Occasionally she paused to ask, 'Do you understand?'

Betty shook her head. While the children explored the house and quarrelled with each other, their mother kept on talking for two hours. She did this day after day, and Betty went to bed each night with her head in a whirl and completely exhausted. However, Betty gradually began to make out what the woman was saying and, in the Lord's grace, after four months she discovered that the young mother was hungry to learn about Jesus.

Later Betty mastered the language sufficiently to be able to lead her to trust in the Lord.

Of course, learning *one* dialect was often not adequate. Sometimes, having learned one, the missionary was needed in another centre where a different dialect was spoken. And most New Villages harboured people who spoke various different languages. Whereas the local people seemed to pick up an additional dialect with comparative ease, the missionary would often feel very frustrated. A mission leader's[23] report on one village asked, 'But what is to be the common language of the new church? To the nucleus of six older

Christians – three Cantonese and three Hakka – have been added one Hokkien, one Cantonese, two Mandarin-speaking Chinese, and one whose normal language is English.'

How they must have regretted the Tower of Babel!

There was no alternative but to settle down to hours of disciplined study every day, and then to go out and practise the new phrases and vocabulary with the neighbours. There would often be peals of laughter as words were muddled or tones reversed. But through all the foolishness of mistakes, gradually understanding and fluency increased and friendships were formed.

It was not just the missionaries, however, who were facing immense difficulties.

◆   ◆   ◆   ◆

Mrs Ho[24]

We sped along the new highway crossing the Central Highlands. Thick virgin jungle covered the steep hillsides around us, while behind them towered the massive Gunong Benom range of mountains nearly seven thousand feet high. Green, green, everywhere – with an occasional splash of bright orange from a cascading creeper adorning a tree. Where the ground was more level, acres of oil palm stretched as far as the eye could see, interspersed with an occasional rubber plantation. Now and then old-style wooden Malay houses, built on stilts, could be glimpsed among a cluster of coconut palms.

The sign back to Kuala Lumpur had read 250 kilometres as we left the small town of Jerantut, at the gateway to the national park. Eighty-six-year-old Mrs Ho had begged us to come and hear her story because she had seen the work of OMF in her town right from the beginning. There were three of us visiting that day in June 2005: Mong, the warm and efficient Home Director of OMF Malaysia, K C, a Chinese friend who had recently retired and graciously volunteered to drive us around the country to meet various Christians, and myself.

Smiling happily, Mrs Ho had limped to the door, dragging her lame leg. Thin and wiry and amazingly upright for her years, her long lanky arms gesticulated wildly as she spoke to us.

When Mrs Ho first came to live in Jerantut there were only three wooden homesteads in the whole area, surrounded by primary jungle. That was in 1940 when she was a young bride from China. When the Japanese invaded China, her parents felt it would be safer for her to marry an overseas Chinese. They could not have known that Malaya would itself be invaded shortly. Young Mrs Ho and her husband faced protracted danger throughout the Second World War and abject poverty as year by year she gave birth to her ten children. Scraping a living as best they could, they struggled desperately to survive.

But Mrs Ho had been brought up as a Christian in China and tenaciously clung on to her faith. She refused to allow her husband to get a job in a gambling shop even when they had no other means of income. Gathering a few children who wanted to learn Mandarin around her, she turned to teaching.

For years she never met another Christian but still she believed, often crying out to God in her loneliness. Struggling against tremendous odds, she tried to live her simple life following God's standards.

After she had endured more than ten years without any fellowship, Peter Murray, a young OMF missionary who had been brought up in China, moved into a town nearby, six hours by crowded bus east of Kuala Lumpur. They rented a shoplot house, one of the many government-built rows of terrace houses, with space for a one-room shop underneath and the area above it for living accommodation. As Peter's wife entered this simple house with a hot corrugated iron roof and a doubtful electricity supply which was to be their home, her heart sank. Would God really be able to call anyone to himself from this remote and backward place?

But God knew all about Mrs Ho and her desperate prayers for help. Working his way from one hamlet to another, Peter eventually arrived at the end of the road – Jerantut. And here at last their paths crossed. What an answer to prayer they both proved for each other.

Every week for 18 months Peter faithfully visited Jerantut. He gathered the children for Bible stories under the trees and played his accordion and taught them Christian songs. As numbers grew, with her energy and forcefulness Mrs Ho was able to find Peter an unused school dormitory where they could hold their meetings. The adults were slow to come, but the children were eager and a regular Sunday School was established.

From these unlikely beginnings 50 years ago, a church has grown up. It has not always been easy. Keith Ranger, writing about an evangelistic campaign he led there in 1971, commented:

> There was real and determined opposition in Jerantut – enough to give real pain of heart to a preacher of the gospel. The message and the Saviour were ridiculed by young men who tore up the gospel tracts and then slunk away on being challenged about it. A non-Christian schoolteacher used classroom time to tell students to boycott the meetings. And a record player was deliberately played at top volume to drown the preacher's voice. In many ways it was a spiritually and physically exhausting week. . . . The great adversary's power could be felt during this

effort in no uncertain way. He undoubtedly succeeded in keeping many people away from the campaign. God, however, was also at work. On one afternoon with only three non-Christians present owing to the schoolteacher's opposition, two of the three professed to take Christ as their Saviour.

How Mong and I praised God that in his mercy, despite all the difficulties and opposition, he has built a strong church to his glory. Today if you visit you will be shown a spacious compound right opposite Mrs Ho's house. The words 'Jerantut Christian Church' are boldly displayed in large letters over the door. The airy upstairs auditorium can hold three hundred people for special occasions, and the regular congregation worships there. Across the wide parking area stands an attractive kindergarten, drawing children from homes of every ethnic background. As they learn about the Christian faith, these children often act as missionaries to their own parents.

Not content with their present progress, the church has just acquired an adjoining empty plot of land on which they hope to build a nursery for three- to five-year-olds. Government restrictions forbid any Christian witness in the regular schools, so Jerantut Church, like many others in Malaysia, is focusing on these younger children.

Talking with the young broad-shouldered pastor, I was impressed by his zeal. He had grown up in Jerantut, trained for the ministry and pastored a church elsewhere. But he asked to come back to his home town because he felt the church leaders still had a burning passion for evangelism into the remote villages. 'It's the legacy of OMF,' he told us. 'We saw this driving goal of evangelism in all their missionaries. And we want to follow their model.'

Over the years Jerantut Christian Church has sent nearly 20 people into full-time Christian work, 14 of whom are still actively involved. This is an incredible achievement for a small remote place.

As we said our thanks and farewells and drove away from the indomitable Mrs Ho, I praised God for women like her. Many of the houses we passed down the street flaunted a scarlet god house by the gate, adorned with prancing dragons. Yes, there is still much work to be done in Malaysia. But, praise God, the legacy of Mrs Ho, OMF and the early Christians is alive and still making an impact.

As Christ promised, 'I will build my church, and the gates of Hell will not overcome it' (Mt. 16:18 AV). Despite all opposition, God's church is being established.

2.

Strategy for Overcoming Difficulties

With all of these formidable difficulties facing the OMF as they began work in Malaya, what strategy did they devise to achieve their goals? How could they hope to see anyone trusting in Christ despite all these problems?

They had only recently come through the 'chastening and humbling experience of the scrutinising fire of Communism'[25] in China. It had been painful and unsettling to have the Communists examine every detail of their work, seeking to destroy it with their criticisms. In China the Christians had been goaded to add their own real or imaginary accusations, so the missionaries often felt betrayed by the very people they loved and had worked to evangelize and disciple. These missionaries had to honestly appraise what they had achieved and to face squarely and learn from their mistakes and failures in order to apply the lessons to the new situation.

'Among the many mistakes to be avoided, two appear to be outstanding,' the leaders agreed. 'As we try to form strong indigenous churches, we must not export our western denominational divisions and it is important that we don't make the young churches dependent on foreign money.'[26]

Initial widespread evangelism

Facing total ignorance of the Christian faith, they determined to saturate an area with the truths of the gospel.
They visited many hundreds of homes in the New
Villages, holding brief conversations and giving out
tracts to any who could read. There was open-air
preaching of the gospel wherever possible, out on the
streets or in the shade of a tree. They handed out invitations to come to meetings in the missionaries' homes, in
the hope that small groups would begin to meet to listen
to the teaching.

Simple lifestyle

The emphasis was to be on simplicity of life. This meant
that the missionaries would live at the same level as the
local people, not flaunting any western advantages they
might have. In this way they hoped not to dominate the
emerging church, but to encourage new believers to take
responsibility right from the start. By living alongside
the people they were hoping to win for Christ, the workers could grow to understand the local viewpoint and
problems. Although they knew it would be hard, slow
work, they trusted that it would pay long-term divi-
dends.

The CIM had sunk large sums of money into erecting
buildings such as hospitals and schools and the substantial headquarters in Sinza Road, Shanghai. This was now
felt to be poor stewardship, because when they were
thrown out of the country they lost all their investments
in the buildings. As it turns out, God had another plan.
When they left China, the mission rented out the premises in Sinza Road to a hospital. In God's amazing grace,

the hospital gave two years' rent in advance, with the proviso that the money must be spent in China. This paid for all the travel costs of the several hundred missionaries to evacuate from inland China and reach the coast. Although God had his purposes for the mission's ownership of large buildings, the sacrificial giving of many supporters was forfeited when the Communists commandeered many hospitals and schools without any thought of reparation. So the mission would not buy any buildings in the new countries, and all missionaries were to live in rented accommodation. 'As we cannot be sure how long we can stay – the political situation being so unstable – that provides a further reason why we should merely rent and not buy,' one of the leaders added.

Only for the new mission headquarters in Singapore was it now felt right to purchase a property; and 33A Chancery Lane served well as a starter. Later this became the Orientation Centre for new missionaries, and then the Discipleship Training Centre, equipping Asian graduates to minister to their fellow Asians. At that point the headquarters moved to a large house in Cluny Road, opposite the botanical gardens.

Finance

'I have never known a CIM/OMF missionary to starve,' Fred Keeble, the mission's treasurer, smiled reassuringly.

I was among a group of new workers listening to him as he outlined Hudson Taylor's policy of looking to God to provide all financial needs. Unlike some other missionary societies, we were never to advertise our wants and, of course, a fixed salary could never be guaranteed.

'All finance that comes into HQ from any country,' he continued, 'is pooled and then divided equally among all the workers. As before when we worked in China, the General Director receives the same amount as the newest recruit. If funds are low, each person will receive less. When more comes in you will have more to enjoy. But we will never go into debt as that would be dishonouring to God.'

Indeed at times our remittance was extremely low and we had to manage on very little. Martin and I lived very frugally in our early days of marriage in Indonesia. Our simple two-room house was furnished with a dining table, some upright chairs, a cupboard and a very narrow double bed. We could not easily obtain western foods like bread and butter, milk and jam, or breakfast cereals, but local rice and vegetables were very cheap. So we had rice, cooked in various ways, for breakfast, lunch and supper. Also, having no electricity meant managing without a fridge or washing machine. However Hudson Taylor's words remained true, 'God's work, done in God's way, never lacks God's supplies.'

Employing local evangelists or other church workers raised a debate again.[27]

'If we employed local co-workers it would make the gospel appear less foreign, and thus could lead to speedier results,' some were heard to argue. 'But foreign money often acts as a snare, even for the most committed convert,' others retorted. 'You are placing a temptation in front of the new believers, to serve God for money not out of love. And what will the non-Christians think? We were charged with creating "rice Christians" in China. We can't afford to give a wrong impression.'

So it was decided not to hire any local Christians to help in building up the church. The aim was for the new churches to support their own workers and not to be dependent on finance from richer countries. Being self-sufficient, looking to God alone, can produce a right sense of dignity and capability. 'I have seen that dependency can often lead to a begging attitude or resentment,' a mission leader remarked in summary. 'This robs a church of God's blessing. All of us, new Christians and old, need to follow our Lord's pattern, who said, "it is more blessed to give than to receive" (Acts 20:35)'.

In the modern age of instant results many find it hard to stick to their principles and persevere through minimal fruitfulness. But this policy of encouraging the national Christians to shoulder responsibility from the start did finally lead to a strong independent church in Malaysia.

A ripple in a pool

'Thinking about the Mission's early methods of evangelism in China,' one missionary observed, 'I feel that those pioneers tried to cover far too much ground. Isn't the scriptural method of evangelism to spread out further and further into neighbouring areas from existing centres of work? That seems to be what Paul did.'[28]

'But that wasn't Hudson Taylor's original plan!' someone else countered. 'He aimed at widespread evangelism. His first step was to place just one missionary couple in each of China's huge provinces.'

'Yes, but I feel that for today it would be much better to establish a central place and then work out from there,' the argument continued. 'This would lead to stronger churches, which could support and strengthen each other.'

This more concentrated strategy became OMF's new policy at the Bournemouth Conference in 1951 when they thrashed out their basic principles. However, in their commendable zeal to cover as much territory as possible, this plan was not always followed.

Church order

Anyone who has sat on a church leadership team will appreciate what heated discussions can arise from differing ideas about worship styles and church structures. Entering a totally new country, it was important that OMF should get this right.

'The believers themselves should work out their own form of government',[29] the mission leaders insisted at their Central Council meeting in 1954. 'If we impose our forms of structure, or leadership style, on the local churches they will resent our domination. So, supposing established churches invite us to work with them, we'll commit ourselves not to start up a new work in competition. We'll aim to build up the Body of Christ in that area.'[30]

'But the mission's main task is to work in totally unevangelized areas. What should happen then?' someone asked. 'Initially there will be no local Christians to choose their own structures. So how will it work out?'

After some discussion it was proposed that the missionaries should thrash out this whole question at their field conference and come to some definite agreement on church order. Once adopted, that pattern should not be changed by an influx of new missionaries at a later date. However, if the *believers* in a local church wanted to change anything they should be free to do so. 'It should be the national believers' prerogative to decide their own form of church government.'[31]

Missionaries are strong-minded people. In an interdenominational mission they come from a variety of church backgrounds which emphasize different teachings. Some want a liturgy or a regular structure to their services, others want flexibility. Some want leadership in the hands of a pastor, others shared leadership. Were they then to be forced to toe the line against their own better judgement? These issues required careful handling.

Finally it was decided that 'every missionary should be free to teach from the Scriptures the mode of church government in line with his own convictions. However, it would be wrong to insist that converts in his area should necessarily follow his own convictions.'[32] If individual missionaries were unhappy with the church order where they were placed, they should request redesignation.[33]

The one exception in Malaysia was in the State of Perak, working from north of Tanjong Malim up to a few miles short of the state capital, Ipoh. Here the mission was welcomed to work with the well-established Anglican Church. All new Anglican workers would be invited to work there, under the local bishop, following Anglican structures and forms of worship.

Challenge to western churches

The excitement of the challenge of the needs of Asia began to spread throughout churches in the West. Meetings were held in which workers described the two hundred million people living in East and South East Asia – only one per cent of which were associated with the Protestant Christian church. Western churches were motivated to rise to this unique opportunity.

Once again, the compelling constraint of the love of Christ was preached to motivate for mission. Emphasis was laid on the incredible fact that Jesus Christ, the Son of God, had sacrificed himself to reconcile the world to God. How could we rob our Lord of the reward of his sufferings by standing idly by? The last command he gave his disciples was to 'Go into all the world and preach the gospel'. Surely the unevangelized peoples of Asia had every right to hear.

The hope of hastening Christ's Second Coming also shone brightly in the hearts of Christians who heard this message. Many felt they might be the last generation which would have the opportunity to take the gospel to these masses.

'As we go forth in faith to these totally new territories,' their leaders argued, 'this will provide an inspiration to the western churches, a challenge and an avenue of service for young people, and a model of faith that where God calls he will also provide everything that is needed.'[34]

Mourning the tragic loss of the opportunity for ministry in the great land of China, the mission gathered its workers together, in faith and courage, to begin all over again. It was a daunting prospect, starting back at the base line once more. An article in *The Millions* commented, 'if this seems a day of small things, let us not be so unwise as to despise it. Great things lie ahead. The Lord has allowed one door to close for the present against us: but a new door is opening.'[35]

Because I was born in China and have always loved this country, I can understand the pain which the closing of China caused to those early missionaries. But I can see now that this situation led to a new missionary concern for Malaysia, and indeed for many countries in the Far East. And China remained closed to outsiders for only 40 years – a relatively short time in the grace and providence of God. And throughout those years God was working amazingly in and through his people in China. Today foreigners find open doors to assist in building God's church in China, as well as in Malaysia and other Asian countries. We can only marvel at God's purposes in history.

3.

Small Beginnings

Between danger and indifference

'My most poignant memory of living in Batu Anam was to return one evening and hear that our seventeen-year-old language teacher had been strangled by the Communists,' Harold Wik recalled. 'It probably was because she was friendly with the European District Officer, not because she taught us. But it may also have been that she had not co-operated with the terrorists in providing food. They were totally ruthless in their actions.'

Remembering those first few months in Malaya, the dangers and the tension under which they all lived came back vividly to Harold.

Harold was a lively American who had arrived in China in 1948, just as the Communists were gaining power. His group had been stuck in Shanghai, unable to travel into the interior, and so had to cope with long, drawn-out disappointment. He was one of the first OMF missionaries to arrive in Malaya in 1951. He and his friend Hayden Mellsop spent a fortnight travelling around Johor State, visiting some of the 66 resettlement areas already established, wondering where they themselves should live. Hayden Mellsop, jokingly nick-named Maiden Hellsop, was a lively Kiwi who remained a bachelor all his life. Once when asked why he never married he replied, 'Why delight one and disappoint a thousand?'

As the two young men visited from house to house, their colourful tracts were often received with smiles and appreciation. But the total ignorance of the gospel or even of the name of Jesus Christ amazed them. Wherever they went, no one seemed to have even heard of the Christian faith.

'We'll have to begin at the very beginning,' was their comment as they wrote home to praying friends. The purer forms of Buddhism as pictured in the West today were not followed at all by the Chinese in Malaya at that time. Their expression of religion was intertwined with traditional Chinese animism. The deeply embedded idolatrous superstition of the local people and their total ignorance of the gospel confronted the missionaries on all sides. This proved a formidable obstacle as they faced the challenge of this new area of work.

Harold and Hayden found that few of the town churches were engaged in village evangelism. The pastor of one large town church told them, 'We have far too much to do among our own flock, and can't possibly spare anyone for the New Villages.' Then he hesitated and added, 'Well, maybe I could spare someone for half a day a week.'

Half a day a week! How long would it take at that rate before anyone trusted in Christ? How easily churches become submerged in their own life and administration.

Entering the first New Village

However, some established town churches were glad of OMF's offer to begin evangelism in the New Villages.

The Reverend George Hood of Holy Light Presbyterian Church in Johor Bahru took a lead here in inviting missionaries to work from his church.

Waiting in Hong Kong were a number of missionaries who already spoke Mandarin Chinese and who were looking for their next sphere of ministry. Among them was Betty Laing, who had taught for three years at the Kunming Bible School in south-west China. In August 1951, Betty and a fellow worker, Doris Dove, were driven by George Hood to Scudai, a New Village some six miles from Johor Bahru. They were the first single female workers to arrive in Malaya and they were welcomed to teach English in the local primary school.

'The school has cleared a room for you two to live in,' George announced as he led the way. They were standing in front of a long white building which housed the school in the centre, while wings on either end held rooms for the teachers. Betty and Doris opened the door, stepped inside and saw a room, 18-feet square, with a kerosene stove, a small table, a desk, three cupboards and two chairs. A curtain was strung halfway across to give some privacy for their beds.

'You won't have your own bathroom and toilet, I'm afraid,' George continued, 'but you can use the school facilities. The children will be in classes much of the time.'

'This will be fine,' Betty assured him. 'When we've unpacked our trunks and hung up some pictures we can make it really home-like.'

But it was not easy living on top of the school. As soon as classes were finished the children crowded into Betty and Doris' room, full of curiosity at these two strange foreigners. Their possessions were examined with great interest, and questions flew back and forth about many of the objects.

While they had been accustomed to privacy in the West, they soon discovered that there was no peace and quiet in a Chinese village. Neighbours wandered in at will and examined anything they saw. Old grannies, left at home to care for the toddlers, would lift the lid of their cooking pot to see what these foreigners ate while commenting loudly to their friends outside. The missionaries often felt as if they were living in a goldfish bowl.

It proved very difficult to find any adult who might be open to their message. The children, however, were interested and friendly. Soon a lunchtime meeting was begun where Betty or Doris would tell stories of how the one true God loved them enough to send his Son to this earth for their sakes. But often the going felt very hard and they wondered how they would ever break through the superstition and ignorance. The power of demonic spirits hung in the air.

The strength of idolatry

At times the atmosphere felt particularly oppressive. How were they to overcome the ever-present forces of darkness? Remembering the words of Jesus that 'this kind does not go out except by prayer and fasting' (Mt. 17:21), they wrote to their prayer partners:[36]

> For these last two days the village has been given over to idolatry. One of the five temples has celebrated an annual festival. Crowds have come from near and far, including many Singaporeans. The first we heard of it was when we were awakened long before dawn by the temple drums.
>
> As we prepared for our usual weekly evangelistic meeting, a little ten-year-old girl, one of our strongest supporters, asked, 'Why are you putting out benches? No one is coming to listen tonight. We're all going to see the show.'

All week it was much the same.

On Sunday we only had eight wee children turn up
while the older ones played marbles outside. One child
shouted, 'We're not coming today!'

'Why not?' I called back.

'We'll come tomorrow,' she replied.

'We don't have Sunday School tomorrow,' I returned
fire.

'Very well, we won't come at all!'

That flattened me.

So they struggled on month after month. 'I find it hard
to believe that the Lord will work here!' one of them
exclaimed in desperation. But the only thing to do was
to cling on in faith that somehow God himself would
work.

Language was also a barrier. The children were learning Mandarin at school so it was easier to communicate
with them. But older people spoke various Chinese languages. So Betty and Doris had to begin language study
all over again. They now tackled Hokkien, as that was
the common language in Scudai. This was a long, labo-
rious process, made more difficult by the tropical heat.
Just when their strength felt totally sapped by the climate and by an exhausting morning teaching, they had
to concentrate on the next language lesson.

Visitors would often arrive, interrupting their study.
Some were local people who just came out of curiosity.
Others came from Singapore churches to see what a
New Village was like. But if they spoke the local dialect
they could be a great help in answering questions about
the gospel, and about the strange foreigners. Sadly, curfew meant that the Singapore visitors had to leave before
most adults had finished their work and were free to
meet them.

Later, when the curfew was lifted, Betty and Doris started meetings at night using a pump-up gas lantern to show Bible pictures. Sitting in the half-dark of the lantern, the crowd would listen to evangelistic talks. But the message was so alien it seemed to fall like water off a duck's back and make little spiritual impact.

With the pressing needs of the many unevangelized villages throughout Malaya, after some time Betty lost her fellow worker and had to soldier on by herself. This was lonely work, but her Hokkien was improving, and at weekends she had the encouragement of visiting George Hood and his family. The school principal and his wife, together with one other teacher, went with her. It felt like a breath of fresh air to worship with other Christians, and George Hood was supportive of all that she was doing.

Wider travel

At George's suggestion, Betty established a pattern of travelling during the school holidays. Loading up her loudspeaker, gas lantern, pictures, posters and song sheets in her old Morris 10 car, she would head north. Being a teacher in the Scudai school made it easy for her to get permission to use a room in any village school. There she would hold Vacation Bible School meetings with the children each morning for five days. And in the evenings she would hold evangelistic meetings using the gas lantern. She found that she could often cover four villages in the month of holiday and be back in time for the start of the following term. Hard work and the determination to grasp every opportunity were very much part of Betty's character.

So the message of Jesus Christ began to spread further afield into other New Villages.

Back in Scudai, some of the older children began to trust Christ as Saviour, but the adults were much harder to reach. Two or three years passed and one day, to Betty's delight, as she entered a classroom she found some of her Girl Guides in a circle with their heads bowed.

'Shhhh!' they said. 'We're praying!'

Could any words be sweeter to the ears of a tired missionary? Betty's heart leapt for joy.

She had undertaken to supervise the local Girl Guides patrol with fear and trembling, not sure if she could manage it or how the local people would react to a uniformed youth group. To her delight, all the girls except one gave their hearts to love and serve Christ.[37] Fruit was at last beginning to emerge.

It was not possible to send other missionaries to Scudai when Betty went on home assignment. She had been away from her family in Canada for six years – three in China and three in Malaya. Missionaries had to be prepared to serve very long terms in those days. She prayed fervently for these few young witnesses who were left to share Jesus with their friends and families.

The small church at Pontian

The fishing villages on the extreme south-western tip of Malaya presented the OMF missionaries with the multiple challenges of remoteness, poverty, unusual living conditions and the constant threat due to the Emergency.

A young Chinese Christian had started the church in Pontian in 1933 by holding meetings in his own home. His father had wasted the family's money on opium so he had never had the chance to go to school. But at the age of sixteen he found a job with a man who was a Christian, and through him came to know the Lord. Throughout the years of the Japanese occupation he managed to draw a small group of Chinese into a church fellowship. For years, this was the only church in the whole district.

David and Jessie Bentley-Taylor were happy to help out while waiting for their visas to Indonesia. David had been known as one of the 'Sons of the Prophets', a group of dynamic young men who arrived in China in the late 1930s. Tall and good-looking, he abounded in enthusiastic energy. Later he became deeply involved in widespread evangelism in East Java, Indonesia, in the midst of a mass movement to faith in Christ.[38]

David and Jessie set off for Pontian in March 1952. Describing the hazardous 35-mile journey from Johor Bahru, David wrote:

> We passed through several resettlement camps, slowing down as we reached the guarded gates. Swamp, rubber plantations, Malay houses among the palms, and the jungle ever close at hand, accounted for most of the scenery. Along the way we met a few armoured vehicles with men holding their guns at the ready. It was enough to bring home the reality of the emergency.[39]

Arriving in Pontian, David's account continued: 'The church leaders, eight men, met us the first evening in the shining new church building. We sat around a square table, upon which I placed a Chinese Bible and they a packet of cigarettes!'

Unlike the situation in the prosperous Malaysia of today, back in the 1950s the few local Christians were very poor. David described a visit to the home of a Mrs

Ping,[40] set on the riverbank amidst an acre of mud and filth with piles of soggy wood chips. They had to duck low under the doorway to get into her room, which was cluttered up with the junk of a decade. Mrs Ping sat on a stool six inches high. Her bare feet sprawled across the doorway, while she wielded a stick to keep the ducklings out. Her bedroom was another dingy cabin with no outside window. But she was delighted to welcome them, and even more so when David promised to obtain a new Bible for her, as hers was falling to pieces. It was a joy to pray together and strengthen her faith in the Lord.

Originally from Swatow, in China, Mrs Ping had become a Christian when her marriage broke up due to her husband's opium smoking. She had been baptized and sailed for Malaya the next day. Her Christian friends had feared that she would lose her faith, and they insisted she take a Bible with her even though she was illiterate. That was 16 years previously, and by sheer perseverance she had learned to read and had read right through Mark and Luke.

These early beginnings seemed insignificant and unpromising as foundations for the future growth of a dynamic church. But in his grace God was to use such people to start a living church to proclaim his good news.

Evangelistic trips

The Pontian Christians had never engaged in evangelistic trips before, but David and Jessie inspired them to begin this new adventure for Christ. Together with David they began to journey out to surrounding villages to preach the good news. Within six weeks of the Bentley-Taylors' arrival, Elder Cheng, Miss K'o and three other women of the church came to pray. David wrote:[41]

> With our little boy Andrew, and two other useful small boys, the piano accordion, the flannelgraph and a bag of tracts, we boarded a bus, a party of ten. We went five miles inland on a road new to us, a dead end, leading to the water locks. At the village of Water Spring Road we stopped alongside the police post where Malays manned a machine gun behind barbed wire.
>
> First we visited the Chinese school, followed by 60 women and children and a few men . . . I preached from a poster, my wife from a flannelgraph, two of the others added a little and we all gave out tracts. We then moved back to the village street, which had about fifty shops . . . In the shade of the covered pavement we pinned up a poster, and I started off again.
>
> I wish I could convey the scene adequately – the long, plaited leaf roof sloping out into the road, the well-stocked shops, the view down the arcade-like pavement, the cobwebs on the beam on which the poster was hung, the rows of children packed in front, the people sitting lazily watching from the nearer shops or across the road in the doorways, the men, rough, swarthy, friendly, stripped to the waist, the women carrying babies, popping in on every side. The Lord certainly helped greatly. . . .
>
> Then we broke up and combed the place from end to end with tracts. We must have had five or six hundred tracts when we began, but at last we ran out of ammunition. By noon we were back home, dripping with perspiration, and my wife is now reading Mark's Gospel with a zealous old soul who comes most days.
>
> Elder Cheng was thrilled at the day's work . . . "That's the first time, the very first time. This church has *never* done such a thing before!"

A village on stilts

An evangelistic sortie to Kukup a couple of months later brought new experiences and showed how the missionaries' enthusiasm spread to the local Christians.

David described it as follows:[42]

> Kukup lies where Malaya ends, on the most southerly point of the whole mainland. There is no church there . . . nor has the Pontian church ever done anything about it until today's sortie. After 11 miles the road petered out into a boulder-strewn track and we found ourselves walking along a causeway with mud, water, shrubs and houses on stilts on either side. At last we stood on the very point, with the sun shining out across the sea to the lovely mountains of Indonesia.
>
> Kukup is built on stilts right into the sea, with a considerable stretch of water, mud and waterlogged scrub between it and terra firma. We walked for fully ten minutes down the main street which consists of three planks, fifteen feet above the water, no handrails but plenty of potholes, crevices, dubious repairs and hazards! Side streets of the same character and altitude ran off at intervals. . . . There are crossroads, small squares, restaurants, shops, homes and temples, as in any other town.
>
> The people stared at our cavalcade, and two young men in luxuriously clean white flannels urged us to go further on. They led us to a wide space fifteen feet above sea level, in front of a temple saying, "This is a place for worshipping God too."
>
> I pinned up two posters, we sang a hymn, and there were not less than 170 men and boys, mostly stripped to the waist, with lots of women, crowding the windows, doorways and shop-fronts. Elder Cheng has come to love this kind of work. This time he spoke and then I followed. . .

> One could not but be stirred by the sea of faces, young
> and old. . . . The Lord's first disciples were humble fish-
> ermen like these.'

So the good news of God's love in Christ was proclaimed in the New Villages and in some more remote
parts of Malaya. Although these early stages of the work
were difficult, the first signs of fruitfulness were beginning to appear. Houses for newly arrived workers had
now been rented in nine places and plans were afoot to
open three or four more centres for evangelism.[43]

While this report rejoiced in the advance of the gospel
through the missionaries, perhaps the even more significant development was that their zeal and sacrifice was
rubbing off on local Christians. They were being
inspired in a new way to take up the evangelistic challenge and not fear ridicule and opposition. Through it
all, the seeds of a truly indigenous church were being
planted.

A hotbed of Communism

One of the new centres was Sungai Chua, 17 miles south
of Kuala Lumpur, with 1,450 families. It was notorious
as a bad area for terrorists. Some years before, the few
Christians had met in the school building each week and
summoned their members by ringing the school bell.
But two years before the new centre opened, the acting
pastor of the church had received a threatening letter
from the Communists. Fearing for his life, he had fled
the village. The bell was silenced and the discouraged
little group of Christians languished without their
leader while the Communist flag flew triumphantly
from the school building. But when Stanley and Nora

Rowe, a lovely hospitable couple who were gifted and dedicated evangelists, arrived to encourage the Christians, the bell could be heard ringing out once more, and regular meetings began to take place again.

Stanley and Nora gave themselves to house to house visiting, distributing tracts and holding regular evangelistic meetings. To their dismay they found that the adults were sullen and suspicious. Having been forcibly removed from their jungle-edged land into this area surrounded by barbed wire, how could they trust anyone? Whisperings and rumours surged back and forth and no one knew who was friend or foe. Out of spite, people might report their neighbour to the authorities as a Communist. So everyone shrank into uncommunicative shells and only a few children came to the meetings. None of them had even heard of Christianity. Moreover, the Communists frequently threatened anyone who appeared interested in this new and foreign religion

No one dared label the Communists as terrorists in case their conversation was overheard. These guerrillas were euphemistically called 'Friends of the Forest' to avoid stating who they actually were. In the all-pervading atmosphere of fear, if anyone glimpsed their illegal activities they would turn a blind eye. The missionaries' house in Buloh Kasap was right next to the perimeter fence. A hole had been cut in the wire behind a large bush, and they would listen to their neighbour's son squeezing through the gap long after dark, returning home for a wash and a welcome meal.

But times proved increasingly difficult for the Communist guerrillas as well. With the heavy rainfall of the monsoon season the jungle could feel pretty grim. Cold nights when they were wet through brought on chills and other illnesses. And the ever-tightening food laws prevented any supplies reaching them.

At this point the government tried a new tactic against them. The Rowes heard planes circling low overhead and finally made out a voice speaking in Hakka calling on the rebels to surrender. The voice promised that they would be leniently treated if they gave up their arms, and many leaflets were dropped with the same message. Nora commented that the most effective way of persuading the guerrillas to come out of the jungle was to have terrorists themselves do the talking over the loudspeaker. Likewise, it made an impact when local Christians themselves shared what Christ meant to them and why they had converted from traditional Chinese Buddhism. Then their neighbours became more responsive. There is nothing like personal experience to carry the ring of truth, especi-ally if it comes from another person from the same background.

Encouraged that a few people were beginning to thaw, Nora said, 'The patient sending of these government messages does have results. And likewise the preaching of the gospel to give sinners peace with God is slowly making headway in the New Villages too.'[44]

Patience leads to a visible church

One hundred miles north of Johor Bahru on the main north-south highway lay the New Village of Cha'ah. Just under six thousand people lived in this resettlement camp, which was known by the British administration as one of the best organized. Hayden Mellsop and Harold Wik had already visited Cha'ah several times to give out tracts and preach the gospel. Winnie Rand and Edith Cork, writing in March 1952, expressed their joy at finding about 15 Christians living there, half of whom understood Mandarin fairly well. The majority of the others were Hakka speaking, so Winnie and Edith launched into learning that dialect.

Before coming, they had prayed specifically that the Lord would prepare hearts for their arrival and that they would see clear conversions early on. So they rented a shoplot house. Sleeping upstairs, they opened the downstairs for visitors. Edith wrote:[45]

> One of us sits in our front room downstairs most of the day to meet those who come. Seeing the English text outside our house, a young Indian came in this morning. He came from Ceylon, and I was able to witness to him and give him a copy of John's Gospel and the tract *Safety, Certainty and Enjoyment*.
>
> By Government ruling we are not allowed to preach or give tracts to the Malays. But quite a number of them read English, so we have posted up a gospel text in English on one side of our door outside, and one in Chinese on the other. We long that the printed word may constrain many to think, and to turn to the Lord.

Unhappily for them, the rainy season brought unexpected hazards. One day floodwaters swept into their camp and within an hour their house was flooded. Hurriedly they moved their stores, books and some trunks upstairs, while the water rose to a level knee-deep downstairs. Anyone who has experienced a flood will appreciate the hard work involved in cleaning up the muddy water afterwards.

At first, they had to hold all meetings in their own home and take responsibility for leading them. But by May 1952 they had seen four people come to know the Lord and a few months later they wrote that

> We have had real joy in seeing local Christians beginning to take responsibility for evangelistic services in different

parts of the New Village. Last week we had a very encouraging meeting in the front yard of one of the Christian families. About 50 people gathered around to hear the gospel.

Soon regular Friday open-air meetings were being held (Friday being the free day in Malaya). The missionaries were encouraged to see 'the boldness with which the Christians witness, even though it isn't easy for them'. Between fifty and two hundred people would come to listen, intrigued by their own neighbours explaining the Christian faith. This helped to dispel the myth that Christianity was just a western religion. The foundations were being laid for the later development of truly indigenous churches, but it took time and patience.

Three months after their arrival, the women were invited to visit the local Old Peoples' Home – a large barn-like building, divided into two dormitories, one for men and one for women, with platforms along the sides of the rooms on which were spread the bamboo sleeping mats. To their joy, a group of local Christians shared this ministry with them from the beginning, helping to sing at the services. Three of them even dared to speak, using different posters to illustrate the stories of Jesus. Winnie concluded, 'Some have since shown interest, but none have yet come to the Lord.'[46]

Attendance at the services gradually grew, largely due to the efforts of the local Christians, many of whom constantly witnessed to their neighbours and friends. Numbers were never large, however. Percy Moore, the OMF Superintendent for the south of Malaya, visited them frequently to encourage and advise.

Knowing the importance of instructing new Christians on sacrificial giving, he suggested that they start weekly offerings. So they hired a tinsmith to make them a box, on the outside of which was painted the Chinese characters for 'He that giveth joyfully will have treasure in Heaven.'

With the nucleus of local Christians growing, just a month later they were able to write, 'November 4 was a great day for the Christians in Cha'ah, for they were formed into a visible church.' Pastor Chou from Kluang, and Evangelist Chin from Paloh, and Percy Moore were appointed as advisers and attended the special occasion. It was emphasized that they were not forming a denominational church but an independent local church. Later the Christians could choose if they wanted to link up with other groups.

Church membership

One of the big problems they faced was who should be accepted as the foundational members of the church. Pastor Chou insisted that 'only those who are clearly born again should be included. They must be already baptized and attending church regularly.'

After much prayer and consultation, the advisers and missionaries only accepted three men and three women who showed real evidence of new birth.

This could have come as a shock and loss of face to the others. So Pastor Chou urged the baptized church members who had not been received, 'Press on in your faith and don't be discouraged. If you show progress you too can be received into membership.'

Happily none took offence, and some came out more clearly for the Lord.

That same evening a service of celebration was held. The six were called to the front and welcomed as the foundation members. Pastor Chou prayed a special prayer for them and everyone rejoiced. The day closed with a delightful party at which tropical fruit, cakes and sweets were served. Anyone else wishing to be baptized was encouraged to hand in their names. Edith concluded, 'Thus ended a very happy day. We trust in course of time many such local churches will be established throughout this land.'[47] Her dream for the founding of a genuinely Chinese church was coming true at last.

The first church business meeting was called a month later. Percy Moore advised that for the time being they keep the organization as simple as possible. A chairman and a secretary were appointed, together with two people to look after the church funds. As is true for all churches everywhere, it was felt important that the money should not be just under one person's control.

The services were still held in the missionaries' living room, but the Christians began to speak of their longing to build their own church. To have a simple building, set apart for the worship of God, would be a silent witness to his presence in their village.

♦   ♦   ♦   ♦

A peep into the future

Fifty years after the establishment of the infant church in Cha'ah, an OMF missionary called Betty Milton discovered the progress that had been made among them. She wrote:

This year God gave me a lovely echo from the past – from 1963, my first term of service in Malaya. An email came via OMF asking if there were any missionaries from the period 1950 – 1970 who had worked in Cha'ah village. I was there 1963–65.

The message came back, 'I think you were my Sunday School teacher.' Christina's aunties had been my Hakka teachers. Christina had come to England to attend some courses and the church elders had asked her to find out [about the missionaries].

Christina herself has been a missionary for over 20 years, first in Mauritius, then in the Mekong area using Mandarin amongst different minority groups crossing borders, and more recently in Central China. Her sister is just about to go to Mongolia.

As she mentioned different families, again and again she mentioned sons and daughters being pastors, church workers and deacons elsewhere in Malaysia and over-seas. I asked how many had gone into full-time service. She said that from the past 20 years or so she didn't know, as she had been overseas herself. But from her generation [there were] about ten.

Cha'ah church only had about 20 members when we were there. There was no secondary school and little employment. We thought of it as a church without a future. What had made the difference?

Christina said two things. First we had set up a link with a Hakka-speaking church in Singapore that had been good for both sides. (All the other churches in Johor state were Hokkien speaking, and the two dialects are mutually unintelligible.) Then she said, 'We had the example right there before us – you missionaries consid-ered the gospel so important you were willing to leave your home countries to bring it to us.'

The Bible encourages us all: 'Always give yourself fully to the work of the Lord, because you know that your labour in the Lord is not in vain (1 Cor. 15:58).

♦   ♦   ♦   ♦

Wide areas of responsibility

While the mission concentrated on placing key workers in the New Villages, sometimes they felt it would be more effective for missionaries to live in a central town so they could evangelize throughout a wider area. The three women working in Kluang, Minna Allworden, Doris Dove and Doris Madden, wrote, 'Our "parish" contains seven resettlement areas, or New Villages as they are now called. The nearest is half a mile away and the furthest 22 miles. To this last place we must go under military escort . . . Picture me with my two fellow workers teaching school in the mornings, visiting New Villages, camps and hospitals in the afternoons, helping with church and Sunday Schools on Sundays, and as you envisage us, *pray*.'[48]

In those days Kluang was a small market town surrounded by dense jungle. In order to combat the Communist guerrillas the British established a garrison there, and the Royal Engineers cleared an airstrip so that troops could be rapidly brought in. A small Anglican church served the army officials and expatriate estate owners, while the Chinese Presbyterian Church and an Indian Mar Thoma Church met the needs of the few local Christians. Town life allowed the missionaries here a comparatively free and more comfortable style of living. They could also build on the foundation of churches that had already been established. The three women were able to rent a small government building as their home and they rejoiced that there were no barbed-wire fences surrounding them.

Kluang Chinese Presbyterian Church was keen to have help from the missionaries. They were facing a problem typical of many town churches at that time. Many of their children were attending English-language schools as this would open up wider educational and job opportunities in the future. But this meant that they could not read or write in Mandarin Chinese, the language used in church worship. Because they did not understand the language used in the services, the young people often became restless and many felt alienated from the church.

The Presbyterian pastor requested that the missionaries set up something for his young people. So among their other tasks they began English Bible classes for these youngsters. From a small group of schoolchildren began a work which was to lead to a major movement, although at the time no one involved could have known how it would grow and develop. As the three ladies prayed and taught, they found other young people who were open to the gospel. They wrote about one of them called Cheng San.

'He was full of earnest questions when he was contacted at a holiday picnic. A week later he came to see us and had a great burden of sin. After he came through to trust in the Saviour, he told us that for some time he had been meeting with a group of schoolboys. They called themselves the private Christians. They met every week to discuss Christianity and read the Bible. On enquiring how it all started, Cheng San replied that his brother had picked up a discarded Bible and was intrigued to read it.'

So we see the power of the word of God to attract and to convict and to point people to Jesus Christ. But at this stage it was still small beginnings and mainly among immature youth. The future growth of the church was still hidden from sight, and those early missionaries had to persevere in faith.

Someone who later was to have a profound influence on the church in Kluang was the outstanding OMF leader Dr David Gunaratnam.

♦   ♦   ♦   ♦

Dr David Gunaratnam

The year was 1960 and Martin, my future husband, had just arrived in Singapore for orientation to OMF and Asia, and to start his language study. As a new missionary, he was asked to speak at the University Christian Fellowship.

To Martin's delight he found that a small group of students met for prayer before the meeting, with an OMF map of South East Asia spread out on the floor between them. Among them was a tall Sri Lankan Malaysian dental student with a wide smile and a gentle manner of speaking. This was the young David Gunaratnam, who was to become our life-long friend.

This particular group of medical and dental students meant business with God. They were being challenged to face the spiritual needs of Asia as week by week they listened to some of the OMF directors expounding God's concern for his lost world. But one recent story was churning round and round in David's mind.

'What does the Christian faith teach?' a Communist cadre had asked.

The reply came, 'Forgiveness, reconciliation both with God and your neighbours, peace of heart through all the storms of life.'

'That's amazing! Show me where that's practised!' was the eager response. 'I'd really like to see that!'

But the Christian could not name a place where this was fully practised, and the cadre went away deeply disappointed.

'We have to be the ones to show them!' the little group's leader, Bobby Sng, exclaimed. 'It's no good becoming church workers and pastors. People think they are paid to spread Christianity. We must go in our professions and live out Christianity in the secular world. Show them it's possible by our lives.'

The group found their prayers turning towards Malaysia and the many small towns and villages which had no Christian witness.

'Most of the churches lie on the west coast', they all agreed. 'But there are hardly any churches up the east coast, where it is largely under-developed.' Risking professional suicide by burying themselves in insignificant places, that is where these gifted young men went. Within a few years Dr David Gunaratnam was stationed in Mersing, a small fishing village on the east Johor coast. Dr Bobby Sng was beginning work in Tanah Rata, high up in the Cameron Highlands. Dr Ng Eng Kee had moved into the small town of Temerloh, which was surrounded by jungle, while others moved, one by one, into other remote, unreached towns.

David came from a Sri Lankan Christian family who had lived in Malaysia for three generations. He had been brought up to go to church, but doubts had often plagued him. 'How can I be sure Christianity is true? There are so many other religions everywhere I look – Hindus, Sikhs, Buddhists – what's so special about Christianity?'[49]

Joining the Christian Fellowship at Singapore University helped to dispel his doubts. Sitting at the feet of Bible expositors like Oswald Sanders, General Director of OMF, or warming to the devotional messages of Arnold Lea, the Assistant General Director, David's faith deepened and grew by leaps and bounds. The gifted OMF evangelist Paul Contento helped him to bring other students to faith, modelling how evangelism might be done. And some newly arrived missionaries like Michael Griffiths inspired him to give his life totally to God.

David became the government dental surgeon for Mersing after only eight months in the more central town of Kluang. Here the small English-speaking Christian fellowship was drawing some high school young people together, ably led by two young teachers – Teo Eng Lin and Khoo Siew Hoon. Realizing that Kluang as well as Mersing needed his help, David faithfully travelled back and forth, making the two-hour journey between the two towns along a twisting road through the jungle. He spent Thursday evening and Friday in Kluang and Saturday and Sunday in Mersing.

How do you start a new church from scratch when you don't know of any other Christians? This was David's prayer as he set up home. God wonderfully led him to an Indian mother who had been praying for a Sunday School for her children. They became the core of his children's work. Other children soon wanted to join in, delighted at the prospect of the young government dentist telling them Bible stories and teaching them songs.

But how could he get adults to come? He found he could hire a hall for between ten and twenty dollars, so he decided to put on some lectures explaining the Christian faith. He single-handedly opened the hall, put out the chairs and arranged everything. He also hosted the different speakers. It was hard work. David Adeney, a dynamic OMF student worker with a Cambridge pedigree and fluent Mandarin, gave Christianity a new status. And when a Chinese student worker, Chua Wee Hian, arrived with a group of Singapore University students to speak, people listened with great respect to someone of their own race.

In his clinic David put out Bible portions and gospel tracts in English and the various local languages. And whenever he could, David shared his faith with his assistant and patients.

To bring anyone actually to make a decision for Christ in such a small and remote town was an uphill struggle. After six years faithfully living and preaching Christ, only a small handful of believers had gathered. Each one was a miracle of God's grace, and especially a teacher called Alan Tan, who came from a very rough background.

'Don't have anything to do with that man,' someone warned David. 'He mixes with a bad lot. They'll ruin your reputation!'

But then Alan confided to David that he wanted to become a Christian. With his usual graciousness David welcomed him into his own home. 'Here I am, trying to build up a church,' he thought to himself, 'and all I can get is a few women and children and now this one very new Christian.'

David came to realize that if Alan returned to his old lodgings his faith might not last for long. His flatmates were deeply into gambling and they could easily have pulled him back into his old ways. If he stayed with David, Alan's life could begin to change.

Because he lived so far away in the little town of Mersing and mixed largely with Chinese people, David's father became concerned about who he would marry. His father suggested several charming Sri Lankan girls. But David hesitated. 'Surely God has chosen a marriage partner for me,' he reasoned. 'And she must be a really committed Christian, not just one in name – someone who will share my goals to bring Christ to Malaysia. And someone who won't be pushing me into always seeking promotion, but will be willing to bear the sacrifice of living in remote places so that a church can be established.'

David's rejection of his father's choice of a bride deeply hurt his parents. How could their lovely loyal son behave in such a way? He had never crossed their will before. So David had to promise that he would not marry anyone except a young Sri Lankan lady of the right caste and education – and these were few and far between in Malaysia.

So the months and years dragged by and marriage seemed a distant prospect for him.

But the Lord has promised to honour those who honour him. One year he was invited to speak at a Scripture Union camp in Penang, which meant he had to travel from the far south east of Malaysia to the far north west. And there at the camp he met Christina.

In later life God enabled David to have a very successful career. He was honoured by the government for his services when they made him a Datok, which is the equivalent of a British knighthood. From the backwater of Mersing, David and Christina have today emerged as outstanding Christian leaders with a key ministry all over Malaysia. Many Christians in Malaysia today owe their faith to David's gracious witness; and his example of holiness and spirituality has challenged many to deepen their walk with God. Because of Christina's loving hospitality, their home has been open to many from all walks of life. As they have loved and cared for their autistic son, their patience and quiet trust in God have been an inspiration to all. People look to David and Christina for spiritual wisdom and guidance. They are outstanding among the many mature Christians whom God has raised up for his church in Malaysia.

4.

Clinging on in Faith

An expanding mission

Steadily the work progressed as OMF missionaries set up homes in one place after another. Annette Harris, Margaret Hollands and Fern Blair moved to Sungai Way in June 1952. This village of five thousand people was eight miles south of Kuala Lumpur. Annette developed into a gifted children's worker. Margaret was a senior worker who appeared formidable – until one got to know her and discovered that she was very thoughtful and full of fun. The following are a few of Fern's memories, fifty years later:

> At the time, it seemed the end of the world: corrugated unlined tin roof, outside toilet, two-storey shop house, with just a thin wooden wall between us and our incense/candle-maker shop neighbours, through which their snoring, breathing, squabbling, hot pepper cooking smells easily came through. In the first few months we had no electricity and had to rely on kerosene for our fridge in all that heat.[50]

However, they lined their walls with preaching posters proclaiming the good news of Jesus, told Bible stories and taught songs to the children drawn to their home by curiosity. They also visited from house to house in the heat of the late afternoon when the rubber-tappers returned from their work. Years later Fern could still remember the sensation of perspiration trickling down her legs as she walked. The shadow of her umbrella never seemed wide enough to cover all of her body.

But in spite of the difficulties they bravely carried on, lone voices in a sea of heathenism. Many villagers were related to the Communist insurgents and so were deeply suspicious of the three women. Danger also came from the Emergency, as several times they heard bullets zinging over their heads. The local British garrison were very solicitous of these three western women living under such hazardous conditions.

'Don't forget to telephone us whenever you need help,' they would remind them. The catch was that there was only one phone in the whole village – and that was in the police station, a five- to ten-minutes walk from their house. And the police station was usually the target for the bullets!

Serdang, one of the largest New Villages (with 1,637 families), was the next community to have a missionary presence. Irene Neville and Ursula Kohler took up residence in Serdang. Ursula was the highly intelligent daughter of a well-known Swiss theologian. I got to know her well later when she also worked in Kluang. There she led a small group of Hakka believers and kindly took our children off our hands once a week. I owed much to her love and support as I struggled in the heat to care for two small children.

When Ursula and Irene first arrived in Serdang they were mobbed by crowds of excited children, but after a while things began to settle down. In spite of having to cope with primitive living conditions, they set about attempting to visit every home, to talk about Jesus and leave a tract.[51] This valiant pair, who had worked together in Kweichow, China and were to spend many years as co-workers, were undaunted by the vastness of the task. They systematically started from rock-bottom to build up a work for Christ.

Suspicion of the foreigners was strong and results were slow in coming, but after 18 months they had a breakthrough. A younger worker staying with them wrote:

> What happened yesterday is a sight I will never forget . . .The ladies had contact with old Mrs Yap soon after their arrival, but it has been only three months since the daughter-in-law came to a meeting. These two heard the gospel and it bore fruit in their lives. Yesterday a group of us walked down to their home – a shabby house with a hard mud floor and one rickety old table. Above the doorway a hideous god (painted on board and costing $1.50, nearly a day's wage) glared at us. On the inside wall were strips of red paper, the cups of offering and the ancestor jar.
>
> I watched those hands, so worn with work, tear piece by piece the strips of paper from the wall. I watched the old woman climb on a bench and take down the god from over the doorway. Together they pulled down the shelves and when they had gathered the rubbish in a heap, added the candles and incense and soaked the board god with kerosene, they took it all outside. It was raining a little and old Mr Yap held an umbrella over his wife as she struck a match and sent the flames devouring the dry paper and kerosene-soaked board. What a sight it was as she stooped there poking the fire to make sure everything was burned. *The first heathen paraphernalia to be burned in Serdang.*

These were sparks of hope in a dark place.

By May 1953, OMF missionaries were living in 15 New Villages in the southern part of Malaya. They were excited to bring the message of the gospel to their neighbours, but they constantly faced enormous difficulties. As well as the debilitating living conditions, other problems abounded. Idol worship was deeply embedded in the Chinese mind and strongly inhibited any openness to the gospel. As Communism increasingly waned, materialism began to strengthen its grip. Local people saw all westerners as English and therefore implicated them in their recent forcible removal from their homes. And then there were the difficulties in communication. The tangle of Chinese languages baffled the newcomers – many were unsure which one to tackle first.

Don Fleming, for example, did a six-month course in Mandarin, then was thrown into a sea of Hakka, from which he was rescued only to flounder in a morass of Hokkien. Commenting on Don's difficulties, the OMF Bulletin concluded 'We hope future experiments will be more successful.'[52]

The missionaries often felt that the odds were stacked heavily against them.

To co-operate or not?

'How can we continue to co-operate with churches which do not teach the need for the new birth and allow unspiritual people into positions of leadership?'

Accusations and counter-charges were flying back and forth in the heated discussion at the South Malayan conference in May 1953. Which local churches are we comfortable working with and where should we draw the line? These were the big questions they were facing.[53]

Before OMF could enter any New Village, they had to negotiate permission from the New Villages Co-ordinating Committee. Although some missionaries had happy fellowship and good working relationships with the existing churches, others felt that the older established missions carefully guarded their spheres of influence, which they had created in earlier days. Even though these missions might not have had workers for these areas, they were still territorial, wanting to keep the areas for themselves.

Sadly, while attempting to co-operate with these existing churches, profound differences of approach became apparent. Three particular areas of frustration emerged: firstly 'the unwillingness of some churches to accept the new birth as a prerequisite of church membership; [secondly] their rejection of a spiritual and disciplined standard of Christian life; [and thirdly] a different approach to the building of the indigenous church.'[54] OMF workers felt that each of these aspects was vitally important. How could they compromise on such essential spiritual issues?

'We must ask for the Co-ordinating Committee to clear more New Villages for our work,' one vocal worker urged. 'Then we can preach the gospel in our own way, and not be shackled by methods we are not happy with. In this way we can form new converts into indigenous churches able to stand on their own feet.'

'Yes,' another replied. 'Wonderfully, increasing numbers of new workers are arriving now, and everywhere I look I see crying needs. Let's focus on the New Villages!'

'But I have been warmly welcomed by the Presbyterian church,' Betty Laing pointed out. 'We shouldn't ignore the opportunities the mainline churches give us.'

Strong feelings were generated on both sides. But amicable negotiations must have taken place, because some time later it was recorded that 'in recent weeks several New Villages have been cleared to the OMF'.[55]

Sungai Ruan, in Pahang, and Mambang Di-Awan, in Perak, were mentioned as examples.

The problem was not yet solved, however, because it stirred up wider issues in the mission's sending countries. Messages began arriving from their North American base, 'How can we keep our supporters on board when they feel we are compromising our position by working with churches related to the World Council of Churches? It's "guilt by association" in their minds. They don't understand the situation in Asia, so each week we hear of individuals and churches withdrawing their support.'

At that time many evangelical Christians, both in Malaya and in OMF's supporting churches, were strongly opposed to the World Council of Churches because of its radically liberal theology and practice. This led to some missionaries feeling very restricted, particularly when describing their work to American churches. They didn't dare to mention with whom they were partnering.

I remember being shocked by a missionary who had been working in Taiwan with the strong Presbyterian church there. He told me that he dare not tell his prayer partners in the USA which local church he was linked with as they felt he should only serve in clearly evangelical churches. But he had been having a very fruitful ministry with this WCC-linked group. The whole situation felt decidedly dubious and untenable – he didn't even feel he could be open with his own supporters.

As the debate raged back and forth, a year later the Overseas Council felt forced to take up a clear position. Due to pressure from the USA, they withdrew membership altogether from the New Villages Co-ordinating Committee. The weight of opinion came down on the fact that it was a sub-committee of the Malayan Christian Council (MCC), the local branch of the World Council of Churches.[56]

However, in the north of Malaya the mission's work came entirely under the Anglican diocese. So the workers there were happy to continue with the MCC.

This debate reflected an ongoing division of opinion within the mission as to whether or not they should relate to non-evangelical churches and movements. And it was not all settled in one direction. In some countries, such as Indonesia, Taiwan and Korea, almost all the mission's personnel worked in and under WCC-related churches, and this proved very fruitful. However in the Philippines, Thailand, Japan and the south of Malaya, OMF planted mostly independent churches, not wanting to compromise their evangelical position.

Opposing viewpoints are not easy to contain in one organization. But such creative tension, when handled wisely, can lead to fresh insights. It says much for OMF's leadership that they were prepared to give each group free rein in their own area. One of the strengths of OMF was that the General Director was not based in a western country but in Singapore, close to where the action was taking place. Each country had its own Director and Field Council, who were free to formulate policy and make decisions.

OMF was a multi-national and interdenominational mission, and such missions have their strengths and weaknesses. Of course it is easier in some respects to work in a team where all the members come from the same ethnic and church background, but this can lead to a narrowness of biblical understanding and cultural expression. An interdenominational international mission like OMF will face fierce debate and even disagreements, which need to be patiently worked through and resolved. But they will be enriched by the input of a wide variety of views.

Taking stock

By 1954, over 50 workers had been successfully installed in the southern area of Malaya. The initial problems had been faced and overcome. The many dialects were being mastered, and the gospel was being preached further afield. But the results were patchy; the danger from the Emergency still made travelling difficult; and overall the work showed relatively little fruit.

The Chinese quote the proverb, 'little tigers become big tigers'. As the workers well knew, most major movements of God start with small beginnings. So they encouraged each other to greater efforts in evangelism and deeper commitment to prayer. Confident that Christ himself is the Lord of the harvest, they hung on believing that great harvests emerge where Christians are prepared to persevere despite suffering and disappointment.

And great harvests have emerged – even though great difficulties still remain.

◆   ◆   ◆   ◆

Pastor Calvin Law Chee Wah

'We had to persevere for a long time over our new building,' Pastor Calvin Law explained to me when I met him in 2005.

'It took seven years of constant, fervent prayer before we received permission to build. We knew we needed larger premises as our numbers were constantly growing. But the months and years dragged by when nothing seemed to happen. Yet God is all-powerful and he changed the authorities' minds. We just rely entirely on God.'

Kuala Lumpur Baptist Church is bursting at the seams. Over one thousand people come to worship each Sunday from many different ethnic groups. So, daringly, they are rebuilding, and this time on an even larger scale. 'There will be five floors,' Pastor Law continued, 'with a spacious auditorium, halls for Sunday Schools, and space for offices. And an extra half floor will be used for parking. We desperately need this space because Kuala Lumpur is such a large, multi-racial city. So we offer services in Cantonese, Mandarin, English, Filipino, Burmese and Korean.'

Pastor Law Chee Wah, responsible for their Chinese work, kindly spoke with me about their church. With greying hair and a slight thin frame, he looked remarkably fit for his age.

'My heart for evangelism grew during my studies at Singapore Bible College in the 1960s,' he told me. 'At that time all the students had to go up country in our vacation breaks and learn from the work of OMF in Malaysia. Our small teams would visit an OMF work in the New Villages and learn all we could from the missionaries.'

His face creased in a bright smile as he remembered those early days. 'We went all over Malaysia, from Yong Peng and Muar in the south right up to Bidor in the north – each vacation working with a different missionary. They didn't have room to put us up so we stayed in the homes of any new believer, sleeping on the floor, washing out the back and eating very simple food. Most of the believers were very poor, you know, at that time.'

'What did you get involved in?' I asked.

'Oh, everything! Children's work, giving out tracts, setting up films to show at night. There were no churches to meet in at that time, so we just gathered the children under the trees. Stanley Rowe would play his accordion and the kids loved to learn the new songs.'

'But how were you received?' I wanted to know.

'They mostly didn't want to listen. We were really not welcome. They would often tear up our tracts and tell us to get out. But we said to each other, "If the missionaries can stick it here, so can we." And the fellowship was great as we encouraged each other and read the Bible and prayed for each other each evening.'

'What do you feel you gained from those evangelistic trips?' I asked.

Once more his bright smile flashed across his face. 'To work hard. And not give up! Even when it is difficult and you see no fruit.

'There was very little response at that time and sometimes we used to wonder at the point of it all. But then we thought, "If the missionaries love the Chinese so much that they are prepared to live under a baking hot corrugated iron roof and live in a house with no electricity in order to bring the gospel to the Chinese, we ought to love our people even more and do all we can to bring them to Christ."'

I could see from talking with Pastor Law that the model he learnt from the OMF missionaries in those early days helped to set the direction for his whole life. A heart for evangelism and a determination not to give up, no matter how discouraging the work, appears to have given him backbone in his young Christian life. And by God's grace this OMF model continues to be a challenge and an encouragement to this day.

Thinking back to those early missionaries I was reminded of the passage in Hebrews which describes the patriarchs: 'these people were . . . living by faith . . . they did not receive the things promised, they only saw them and welcomed them from a distance' (Heb. 11:13). Yes, Christian ministry must often wait for results. But the results will surely come.[57]

5.

Contributing to the Anglican Church

Twelve men in dark suits were seated around the long oval table of gleaming dark polished wood. The stern portraits of former CIM directors gazed down on the nervous candidate as he faced the questioning of this august committee.

'Having completed your Anglican theological studies, how do you feel about joining an interdenominational mission?' Reverend George Scott, an ordained Anglican who was the British Home Director, asked the question.

Hesitating a little because at that stage he hadn't yet thought it through, the candidate replied, 'Although I am an Anglican I don't want to export my denominational emphases. I am not particularly interested in denominations.'

'You've given the wrong answer!' smiled George Scott, and the room erupted in laughter. 'We are an interdenominational mission. Not non-denominational. We want every member to contribute positively from their own church backgrounds. Anglicanism has much to give to the whole body. Also, just stop to think for a moment. It is impossible to plant a church which is devoid of particular theological emphases, worship styles and leadership patterns. We all carry our own backgrounds with us, and new Christians overseas will inevitably be influenced by the more mature Christians who planted the church among them.'[58]

Happily this candidate was accepted in spite of not having thought through his position. Martin Goldsmith later became my husband.

The Overseas Missionary Fellowship of the CIM worked this principle out in two ways. In countries where their members were from a variety of church backgrounds, each worker brought their own contribution. On the other hand the mission also felt free to have one area which was exclusively Anglican, following the pattern developed many years before in Szechwan, China.[59] OMF approached various dioceses in the new countries they were proposing to enter to ask if they were willing to set apart an area for their Anglican workers to cover. Some dioceses hesitated, feeling the mission was too evangelical. But the Diocese of Singapore and Malaya, which by now had their own Chinese Synod, kindly invited OMF's Anglican workers to join them in the Parish of South Perak.

Because it had previously been under British rule, Anglican chaplaincies had been set up in key towns in Malaya. These were originally to serve expatriates, but gradually reached out to the local population as well. So the Anglican Church was well established by the time OMF arrived in Malaya.

Sadly, working exclusively with the Anglican Church could lead to the mission being cut off from the main denomination in the north, which was Methodism. But even so it was felt right to set up this Anglican area and the missionaries had complete freedom to develop their own type of work.

Reverend George Williamson provided wise and gracious leadership for the OMF team. Warm and genial,

George was one of the experienced 'old China hands'. The task of negotiating with the bishop about how his workers might fit in with the diocesan plans fell to George. They offered him an area in Perak State, which stretched some 90 miles from the town of Tanjong Malim northwards to about ten miles short of the state capital of Ipoh. The twisting, winding road from the state border passed through thick rubber and jungle up through centres like Slim River (named after Field Marshall Slim), Trolak, and Bidor. There it entered the south end of the Kinta valley, at that time one of the richest dredge and open-cast tin mining valleys in the world. Some twenty-five to thirty New Villages were situated either on or near this main road. In none of them was there any Christian witness.[60] It was a challenge that needed to be embraced.

The new missionaries received a very warm welcome and every encouragement and assistance from the diocese. They felt a kindred spirit with many of the Chinese clergy and congregations. The Anglican church in Ipoh even gave them a freewill offering and added that their lady worker was willing to help with the Cantonese work in Bidor.

After studying the situation, George Williamson decided that their aim should be to open strategic centres from which evangelism and discipleship training could spread. Tapah proved to be the obvious centre for the work, both from a geographical and administrative standpoint. But at first it seemed impossible to rent accommodation there.

God had his hand on the right house, however.[61] Unexpectedly, it came through a sudden bereavement. Sometimes in answering our prayers God demands from us a sacrifice. An Indian family in Tapah had been praying for missionaries to come to their town for a long time.

When the husband died suddenly, the wife and two daughters moved to live with relations. They heard about OMF's needs and offered to rent their home in the centre of the Tamil district to OMF. Grateful for this provision, the Williamsons, who had their eyes fixed on the Chinese, now realized that God wanted them to broaden their concerns and help the Tamils too.

They launched into the work with enthusiasm and regular Tamil services soon began, along with Sunday School for Indian, Chinese and European children, and an English-language service. As usual, it was the children who attended at first. The missionaries had to be very patient, waiting for the adults to follow.

The New Village of Bidor

Bidor, with a population of over ten thousand, is situated about a hundred miles north of Kuala Lumpur. Bidor was the first New Village in the Anglican area that we entered. The new workers discovered that the business people who lived on the one street of shops were largely Cantonese, while most of the rubber-tappers, tin mine workers and vegetable growers were Hakka.

Marion Parsons, an indefatigable worker from the British west country with a Bristolian burr, led the team. Ruth Dix and Ethel Barkworth were stout-hearted companions. When I met Ethel in her later years, she appeared at first to be unsmiling, prim and proper. It must have required great grace for someone raised with stiff British etiquette to adapt to the rough and tumble of a newly forming Asian community.

After some searching, these three ladies were able to rent a new shoplot house on the main road.

Ethel wrote:

> We are becoming accustomed to the daily peak temper-
> ature of 90° – 94° in the mid-afternoon [they had no elec-
> tricity for fans] . . . even the jarring of broadcast jazz,
> which may be heard from five loudspeakers simultane-
> ously (three at very close range) is not as jading as at
> first. We now scarcely notice the cocks, which may crow
> at any hour of the twenty-four, save when a rooster takes
> up his position within five yards of one's pillow . . .
>
> But God forbid that we should become hardened to
> things that grieve his heart . . . when the air is filled for
> minutes on end with the cries of a child who is 'getting
> it' from a tough stick in the strong arm of an enraged
> mother; or when a woman discloses to us the pain in her
> heart because her husband has taken another wife.[62]

The local people showed little curiosity about the westerners living among them and even seemed chary of
asking them any questions. In fact, the villagers were
very suspicious of each other. Each family kept itself to
itself and the different dialects deepened the divisions
among them. The older folk held tenaciously to their
customs of burning incense, lighting candles and offering paper money, as well as wine and food, to the ancestral tablets.

A director commented: 'Speaking humanly, it would
appear that three missionaries dumped down in this
atmosphere and living here for three months have not
made even a ripple in the pond.'[63] Patience and tenacity,
coupled with a deep faith in God, were constantly called
for. The odds seemed hopelessly stacked against them.

And, yet, a few people were being touched by their
message. The local headmaster, who had attended a mission school in his youth, showed some interest. The

businessman who taught them Hakka began asking questions about their faith, and a man to whom they lent two Gospels and *The Life of Hudson Taylor* began to see how Christ challenged his own religious beliefs. These were tiny rays of hope to which Marion, Ruth and Ethel had to cling as they prayed in faith for definite conversions. With hindsight we can see that the gospel was more likely to appeal to those who were educated.

Just like the workers down south, Marion, Ruth and Ethel set themselves the task of visiting everyone in the village, going from house to house. Wherever opportunity was given they explained the gospel story and left a Gospel and simple tract if someone in the home could read. The labyrinth of lanes and tiny houses constantly surprised them, revealing more and more homes. Once a week they would fix a gramophone onto the carrier of one of their bikes, add a basket of Gospel Recording records and a large bundle of tracts, and set out for another village. Between them they hoped to reach several mining estates and other villages where the gospel had never been preached before.

After spending two years living and working in Bidor, Ethel Barkworth described some of the problems they were often up against:

> 'Please would you put in a word for me with the government official?' someone would ask. When we remonstrated that we had no authority there they would reply, 'But are you not British? You're agents of the government, aren't you? Come to spread the westerner's religion?'
>
> A few weeks ago I was caught in a downpour and while I was waiting someone remarked to me, 'I suppose your salaries are paid by the government?' [But] the misunderstanding gave the opportunity to tell from

whom we received our commission and of his Fatherly love.[64]

When Ethel offered a tract to an old man working in a tin mine, he asked her, 'Is this *Heavenly Lord Hall* or *Gospel Hall?*' (meaning Roman Catholic or evangelical).

'It's gospel teaching,' Ethel replied.

'Ah! That is from England and *Heavenly Lord Hall* from another country, is it not?'

He was caught by the popular misconception that each country and people has their own religion. A Malay is a Muslim, a Punjabi a Sikh. It had never entered his mind that one religion alone might be the truth and so should be followed by all races.

But the missionaries in Bidor had their own secret weapon.[65] They wrote, 'Each Wednesday when we gather after breakfast for morning prayers, we open the Mission Directory to be reminded of the names and stations of all our workers in Malaya. Heading the page stands the promise of God, "*As the garden causes the things that are sown in it to spring forth, so the Lord God will cause righteousness and praise to spring forth before all nations.*"' And with that promise in mind they prayed fervently to God for the new life of the gospel to break into their town.

Ethel Barkworth's articles in *The Millions* give us a good picture of life in a New Village and the spiritual calibre and tenacity required for someone to stick it out year after year. She lived very frugally but was extremely generous to others. As a skilled nurse she touched many lives and her quiet disciplined life was a gentle model for others to follow.

Another year passed and Margaret Heale, a nurse who had been sent to join the team in Bidor, wrote, 'After three years of missionary work, not one adult of over twenty-one has been saved.' It must have felt very discouraging, considering all the hard work and faithful prayer, which they had poured into the area.

Medical care opens hearts

Other workers, however, were trying a new method of evangelism. When the New Villages had been set up, the government had built neat Red Cross bungalows and clinics in each one, with a resident nurse in a central station. When the Emergency was more fully under control, the Red Cross wanted to withdraw all their nurses and hand over the medical care. In September 1954 Dr Max Gray, an experienced OMF missionary, was asked to take responsibility for the clinics in seven New Villages in the northern part of the Anglican field. He soon moved into Mambang Di-Awan. Then, in January 1955, he began work in seven villages in the Bidor area as well. Prayer went up that offering medical help might break down barriers and suspicion.

Once a fortnight the doctor's familiar white Land Rover, presented to him by the Red Cross, drove up to the Treatment Centre. Eager hands unloaded the medicines which the doctor's wife, a pharmacist, had spent hours pounding and making up. All the equipment was arranged on a long wooden table, while a few benches were pushed together for the patients to sit on as they waited. Curtains were drawn across the windows to give some privacy, and the doctor welcomed the patients one by one.

There were up to 50 patients to be seen each day. While they were waiting, one of the Christian workers showed a gospel poster picturing a Bible story and explained some simple spiritual truth. They taught waiting patients catchy Christian songs as well, with words which were easy to remember. And each patient was given a tract with a word of explanation before they left.

In spite of all the medical care and love shown, Margaret commented, 'We do not find a ready acceptance of our message, but rather a hard wall of resistance due to suspicion, fear of intimidation (by the Communists) and often a desire only for material prosperity. Nevertheless, the weapons of our warfare are mighty through God to the pulling down of strongholds. We believe that in each village there are people to whom God is speaking, and that in due time we shall reap, if we faint not.'[66]

Her perseverance and faith shine against the background of indifference.

Gradually, suspicion began to be broken down. An elderly Christian who had been converted long before, in China, developed cataracts and became blind.

'I'll take you to hospital,' offered Dr Gray. 'It's likely they can help you see again.'

His friends and neighbours were sceptical. Who has ever heard of a blind person being able to see again? But the patient had the courage to trust Dr Gray. The operation was successful, and he caused a great stir when he came back to Bidor with his sight restored. Maybe, people began to think, these foreigners did have something good to offer after all.

George and Phyllis Williamson, who had settled into the Indian home in Tapah, described their first three years as 'digging and seed sowing' because much preparation was needed before any adults responded. However, each Sunday their front room was filled with school-aged children who loved the Bible stories and unashamedly sang the songs they were learning wherever they went.

'What is this song about fishers of men?' a Hindu father asked, and Phyllis had the joy of explaining the story to him.

Trying every method they could think of, the versatile missionaries started a smaller group for older teenagers meeting after the Sunday School. And there was great joy when two of them were baptized and three confirmed.

'We must get them to meet other Christians so they know they're not alone,' George commented. Quarterly Youth Days for the area, some in English and some in Chinese, were started. A European government official kindly put his home and garden at the Williamsons' disposal. Here lively programmes of games and Bible study were held.

Other methods were also tried out: evangelistic Christmas parties, English classes, cookery lessons, film-strips, lending libraries – anything that might draw people in.

'Please pray for me,' Doris Tan, a member of their youth group, wrote after she had moved to a remote area. 'There are no other Christians here and I feel so lonely. But when I'm down I sing some of the songs we learnt and read my Bible, and that's a comfort.'

It was hard to be a Christian in those early days when so few were open to the message.

After supervising the Mission's Anglican work for three years, George Williamson was pleased to comment:

> Three missionaries started in one village, then two in a small town – 'digging' literally and metaphorically! We have seen a work expanding, with twenty-three workers now, living in six villages and two towns – 'seed sowing'. We are beginning to see consolidation and a small

harvest – 'reaping'. May the harvest be gathered in before the rains and storm clouds break to destroy the precious grain.[67]

Always, the threat that their time in Malaya might not be long hung over their heads. They must buy up every opportunity, following the example of Jesus, who said, 'As long as it is day we must do the work of him who sent me. Night is coming when no one can work' (Jn. 9:4).

Hard times for new missionaries

Life continued to be challenging for each group of new missionaries who answered God's call to meet the spiritual needs of Malaysia. And local Christians, too, faced enormous opposition and were often isolated from family and friends. It was into this situation that Denis and June Lane arrived in April 1960. Denis later became Assistant General Director for the whole of OMF. Their early days were far from easy and show clearly how difficult life could be. Denis studied for a degree in law before being ordained as an Anglican minister. He then served curacies both in London and Cambridge before answering God's call to work in Asia.

One day Denis and June were sitting in the OMF Language Centre in Singapore, listening to a missionary just about to leave for her first furlough.

'What will life be like for us?' they wondered as they eagerly settled down to listen to Minna Allworden. Denis' careful legal mind longed to know more details about what the future might hold.

But what a shock! 'I've been in Gemas Bahru New Village for four years, working day after day and often late into the night,' Minna said, and her eyes began to glisten with tears. 'In all that time there were only five believers. And then, one by one, they stopped coming. The last one went back to his old superstitions last week and now there are no Christians left.'

Stunned, June and Denis looked at each other. Was that what they had ahead of them? Could it really be that OMF had been in Malaysia for nearly ten years with so little fruit?

When I visited Denis and June recently in their bunga-low in Worthing, it was hard to visualize the contrast of the story they told me about their first years in Malaysia.

Shortly after finishing at the OMF Language Centre, June and Denis took the long train journey north with their toddler son Andrew. Reverend Don Temple, super-intendent for the Anglican work, welcomed them to the small town of Tapah. Don had come to the railway sta-tion to meet them, but his car was so small that with all the luggage there was no room for Denis. He had to sit on the tailgate with the boot wide open as they chugged along the road for two miles out of town.

At last they reached the old estate bungalow which Don and Olive had been able to rent for their own living quarters. It was dilapidated and surrounded by rubber trees. Next to it stood three disused police huts, which had been used during the Emergency for protection of the estate manager. Each consisted of a simple wooden room, ten feet square, with a corrugated iron roof. The hut at the end was too decrepit to use, but Denis and June were given the other two rooms as their home. One room contained a double bed; the other had a table and two chairs and they added Andrew's cot. After the com-parative comfort of a three-bedroom curate's house in Cambridge, this was to be their home.

Denis faced an internal struggle. With his middle-class upbringing he felt deeply responsible for his wife's comfort and well-being, and yet as missionaries they were willing to live a life of sacrifice. But such living conditions were not what he had imagined.

June was not able to cook for her own family, as there were no facilities, so they had to take all their meals with the Temples. They had to walk across to the main house to give Andrew a shower or use the toilet. Don and Olive had strict ideas about bringing up children and commented freely to the younger couple about their methods. The older missionaries had survived very primitive living in China. So if Denis or June remarked on the difficulties they were facing, they were told firmly, "You are in Malaysia now. Toughen up!"

As they continued their reminiscences, June laughed and said:

> That was my first encounter with snakes! You see, the rubber trees grew right down to our huts and the snakes loved it. There was a drain running along the back to catch the monsoon rain. One day when I was carrying little Andrew in one arm and a basin of water to wash him in the other, a cobra came out of the drain and reared up at me. Panicking, I threw Andrew at Denis and the bowl of water at the snake! The snake disappeared, but after a while someone complained that every time they went into the small bathroom they heard a hissing sound. Sure enough it was the cobra again! Denis valiantly tried to strike it, leaping out of the door afterwards. Trying to follow him, the snake poked its head out through a knothole in the flimsy wall and spat at Denis. Fortunately he was wearing glasses and so the venom did not reach his eyes. And there the snake got stuck. Grabbing a stick, Denis managed to kill the cobra as it swung back and forth in the hole. But we were all badly shaken.

I smiled as I tried to picture this incongruous situation: a bespectacled Anglican clergyman doing battle with a large venomous snake swinging from a knothole in the door!

'But there were not only snakes,' June continued. 'There were huge eight-inch centipedes, great reddish-brown ones with a sting that could kill a baby. They used to drop down unexpectedly from the roof. That was fine if you could see them. But of course we had no glass in the windows, only netting. In a storm – and in the rainy season the storms came nearly every day – we had to shut the shutters to keep the rain out. As the electricity only came on at 7 p.m. it was too dark to see the centipedes!

'What scared me in town,' June continued, 'were the dogs. They were really wild. There were packs of them roaming the streets, scavenging for what they could find. I dreaded going to the market.'

'Life in Slim River wasn't much better,' Denis sighed. 'We moved there after six months. At least we had a home of our own. But it was very simple: slatted wood walls, corrugated iron roof and an old Valour kerosene stove which spewed black smoke over everything. We were right next to the railway line, and the clanking of the night train woke us up at 2 a.m. without fail, until we learnt to sleep through it. On our other side was a rubber factory – the smell they produce is unbelievable. June was pregnant with Christine just then and used to walk around with a hanky dipped in eau-de-cologne over her face to keep from being sick.'

'And when she was born, Christine was constantly ill,' June added. 'She developed renal acidosis and couldn't keep any food down. I was so worried about her as she was underweight, and I didn't know who to go to for help. Dr Max Gray, our OMF doctor, lived 40 miles away. Anyway I couldn't phone him, as we had no phone. There was only one phone in the village and that was at the Post Office, right on the other side of town. So we didn't manage to contact him.

'While Christine was still on four-hourly feeds I remember trying to give her her 2 a.m. feed. Every night a rat came out and sat on the rafters opposite, watching me. It was so eerie!'

'The odd thing was,' Denis added, 'our house was in the Indian section. It was a Hokkien village, and we were learning Cantonese. So we didn't get much language practice. Language learning provision was pretty thin in those days.'

In Tapah, our first home, our teacher was a fifteen-year-old boy who had never had to teach anyone. We had an old primer and one more up-to-date book, but all we did in those six months was learn to distinguish the tones. When we moved to Slim River our situation improved. There was a competent schoolteacher to help us. At last I was able to attempt my first sermon. I had to go through it with my teacher word for word, and then learn it off by heart. To my consternation, only one man turned up for the service – and he spoke Hing Hwa! I don't know if he understood, but I gave it to him all the same.

Our most promising Christian was a Tamil from the labour lines called David. Eric Roberts, another missionary, had helped him with his education and the passing of exams. David did well in his studies and eventually felt called to the ministry. He trained at Trinity College in Singapore. Unfortunately he went away from his evangelical convictions in the pressure of a liberal theological college. It can be very discouraging when something like that happens.

Coping with missionary life in such situations demands a great deal of commitment and perseverance.

There were some who found the going too tough. But even so they made a valuable contribution.

♦   ♦   ♦   ♦

Jimmy Chee Boon Soo

'But they didn't all survive!'

The speaker was a veteran missionary in her eighties who had watched a large number of OMF missionaries pass through Malaysia. Looking at her silver hair and gentle manner, I was surprised how forcefully she spoke.

'I found OMF very rigid. They had their goals and you had to fit in. For instance, they said you must learn the language. And this was very desirable. But some found they just couldn't master the Chinese tones and their ways of expressing things. They never really got the language.

'Also, it was appallingly difficult to go from house to house trying to give out Christian tracts when no one wanted you. The Chinese stared at you with such hostility. And the heat was awful – even with an umbrella the sun seemed to blaze down.'

Once more she repeated: 'Some just couldn't take it. It was a real waste.'

She looked at me candidly. 'We had two breakdowns near us. One was such a brilliant teacher. She would have done fine in a town. But the Mission had their calling to the New Villages and wouldn't hear of it. And there was a gifted carpenter who could have taught carpentry in the city and made a real impact. He was a square peg in a round hole in our New Village. It just didn't suit him.

'Oh yes,' she added, 'and there was David and Thelma Priston. They should have been placed in a town

– that would have suited them far better. Not everyone can cope in a village.' And then she continued with a little laugh, 'I felt a huge sense of release when I left to get married, and wasn't stuck in a village any more!'

'David and Thelma Priston' – I vaguely remembered them leaving Malaysia and returning to UK. But at my very next interview in Kuala Lumpur I heard David Priston's name again. Energetic visionary Jimmy Chee, personal assistant to the Anglican Bishop of Kuala Lumpur, had become a Christian in his teens through David Priston's ministry. As I listened to his story I thought, 'If Jimmy Chee had been the only person the Pristons had influenced in Malaysia it would have been worth coming for this young man.'

David had been out in the heat visiting from house to house in Slim River New Village when he met the young Jimmy. Jimmy had never known real love from his own family and he found friendships at school difficult. But in David he discovered someone who was actually interested in him. So he began visiting the Pristons' home, initially to improve his English. But it was their warmth which drew him to their home. He had never met such a loving welcoming couple, or seen such a deep relationship between husband and wife.

After some time when the trust between them had grown, David read Psalm 23 with Jimmy. He explained how God wants to be our shepherd and care for us. Seeing God's love and acceptance so vividly in David and Thelma's friendship helped Jimmy to make his decision to become a Christian.

Jimmy's parents strongly opposed his interest in Christianity. Yet as they watched him they saw a miracle happen. They had always believed that making their son perform the daily ancestral worship would turn him into a well-behaved boy. Gradually they came to realize that whereas the ritual performed year after year was a total failure, Christianity was having a remarkable influence. Jimmy grew more helpful and loyal as his Christian faith deepened. Although initially his parents forbad him to become a Christian, after much prayer and patience on Jimmy's part they finally agreed. And to Jimmy's delight, when he was baptized his parents donated a pew to St Paul's Church Slim River to show their appreciation.

David made time to do Bible study with Jimmy, emphasizing the Bible as the foundation of all we believe. He gave Jimmy his first Scripture Union Daily Bible Reading notes, and to this day Jimmy has never failed to follow them.

Sadly, soon afterwards David and Thelma had to return to UK, but Jimmy now found himself nurtured by the next OMF missionary, the lively, humorous and academically brilliant Dr Alan Cole. Alan urged Jimmy to move to Kuala Lumpur to further his studies, and there he stayed with Peter Young. Peter had recently resigned from OMF in order to be free to do English-speaking work in the towns. So the chain of missionaries grew who had an influence on Jimmy's life. Looking back years later, Jimmy could count more than ten OMF couples and various single women who had challenged him and blessed him spiritually.

Slight in stature but bursting with energy, Jimmy's gifts lie in organization and administration. While still a student he would worship at the central St Mary's Church in the mornings, faithfully teaching their Sunday School children. Then after a brief meal and rest he would cycle to St Gabriel's School and help Peter Young set out a room for the new English language service he was starting. During the vacations when he travelled north to his home, Jimmy threw himself into helping the OMF Anglican missionaries in their evangelism in many different villages, and each Sunday he translated the service at St Paul's Church, Slim River into Hokkien.

Jimmy started his first job as the chief payroll officer in the remote Rompin Iron Mine, Bukit Ibam, Pahang. Here he coordinated the monthly services when the vicar from Kuantan came to minister. He himself taught Sunday School for some 60 local and Australian children using Scripture Union materials.

Moving on to Kluang, Johor, he ploughed through the long course of study so as to qualify as a Lay Reader, encouraged by Reverend John Lousada, an Australian CMS worker. Throwing himself into the new opportunities, he not only led Anglican services on Saturdays but also helped Henry Guinness, an OMFer working in the Presbyterian church, on Sunday evenings with his service. Sometimes he also accompanied him on his village evangelism. Ever on the lookout for an opportunity to serve God, he noticed that the Mar Thoma church offered very little for their children. So he hired a bus at his own expense to collect 40 or 50 youngsters from the Mar Thoma and Anglican churches and bring them to join the Anglican Sunday School which he ran. The youth fellowship was also in his care, and eventually two of their members were ordained into the ministry.

Today, the list of Jimmy Chee's administrative responsibilities is very long. He has served as personal assistant to Bishop Lim Cheng Ean since the year 2000. He is their communications officer, sits on the properties committee and the salaries commission, is a member of the archbishop's advisory board and served on the inter-diocese council for the creation of the Province of South East Asia. He was also chairman of the board of governors of the Pudu English Girls School for some years and is at present a member of the Malaysian Theological Seminary council and of their personnel committee. Jimmy has been a synod representative for over 30 years and helps to co-ordinate mission works between his diocese and the diocese of Lichfield, England.

With all of these commitments, it was heart-warming to hear him describe his feelings about the opportunity to visit England. His face broke into a wide smile as he said, 'I was excited at the thought of meeting David Priston. I had been praying and praying that it would be possible. And God brought us together. I was so happy to see him again because I owe him so much.'

No, the missionaries did not all survive, but God's work through them continued. As the prophet Isaiah wrote, 'The grass withers and the flowers fall, but the word of our God stands for ever' (Is. 40:8).[68]

6.

Hopeful Signs

Though progress was often painfully slow, perseverance and faithfulness began to bear fruit. It was only when the Lanes were posted to Teluk Anson (now called Teluk Intan), after more than two years plodding on in the heat, that Denis at last began to feel he might have something to contribute. At this stage June's energies were totally absorbed in looking after the children and the home. Reverend Bob and Amy Harper, 'old China hands', were in charge of St Luke's Church in the town. They held services in both Chinese and English and had a small congregation of 25 to 30 people – Chinese, Indians and Eurasians.

The mission was still focused on the New Villages, and so Denis was asked to be responsible for evangelism in three outlying villages: Batu Duabelas, Langkap and Chui Chak. These villages had been formed during the Emergency and Communist influence was still strong in some of them.

By now Denis had been able to buy a little Austin 7, and so with the help of some Teluk Anson Christians, he began evangelism in Batu Duabelas. It was easy enough to gather children, but adults hardly ever came. And once the children were about ten years old, he found that they too stopped coming.

Because of the strong Communist influence, only one adult became a Christian in Batu Duabelas. He was so poor he only had a table, a bed and a stool in his one-room shack. Yet when they left, this man gave Denis a present of $1, a sacrificial sum, in gratitude for what he had learnt. Denis was greatly touched by this loving act.

In Langkap, the next village, Denis was delighted to find a young tailor called Lai Yong Thai. Some years before, he had been converted from gangsterism to Christianity in Singapore when he had gone to a meeting in order to disrupt it. God had laid his hand on him and saved him. Lai had a great sense of humour, a longing to share his faith with others, and he spoke fluent Hakka, Cantonese and Mandarin. So he proved a wonderful help. Lai owned only half a shop (the other half housed a coffee shop), but he was very willing for meetings to be held in his half and he invited a number of his friends who frequented the coffee shop to attend. So gradually a weekly Bible study began to grow there.

Sensing what a difference Lai could make, Denis asked him if he would go with him to Chui Chak, the third village for which Denis was responsible. Denis remembers them setting off in his little car and then stopping in the middle of a paddy field with the mosquitoes buzzing round, praying and asking the Lord to guide them. They had no idea how to begin or what to do. They started by giving out tracts and telling Bible stories illustrated from a large picture roll.

When they visited the village headman, he introduced them to a young man who had bought a Bible from the Anglican team some time before. This team, from Teluk Anson, would go out sporadically to different villages and hold an open-air meeting. Because there was no television or entertainment in the villages many would turn up to listen, and Bibles and other Christian literature would be sold. Then on return visits they could follow up any interest that might have been generated. This was how Denis and Mr Lai first came across the young man.

In spite of all their teaching, this particular young man vacillated between Christianity and Communism and never came to faith. But one day, when Lai and Denis were visiting him, another man who kept ducks came in. He was very agitated and told them that so many of his ducks had been stolen he was forced to sleep next to them each night. 'But I'm so afraid of the demons that prowl around in the dark, I daren't sleep there!' he exclaimed. 'What shall I do? Someone might come and steal all the ducks I have left.'

After Lai explained to him that the Lord Jesus has power over all evil spirits and would keep him and the ducks safe, he finally agreed, 'If your Jesus can scare away the demons I'll believe in him.'

He became the first believer in Chui Chak as he experienced for himself the power and the love of our Lord in his difficult situation.

Although they felt inadequate, Lai and Denis continued their evangelism together. Lai had a striking gift of humour that would set people at ease. Denis would play his accordion and sing gospel songs. As they prayed, each week they found God leading them to one person who was willing to listen. As was so often the case, the results seemed very small and it took a great deal of perseverance to keep going out to the villages.

One day Denis asked Lai if he felt embarrassed about working with him because anti-foreign sentiment was running high. He replied that if Denis had gone visiting alone, no one would have listened to him as a foreigner.

If he himself had gone alone, no one would have listened to him as a mere tailor. But they gave each other face and acceptance. This gave Denis a deeper insight into Chinese culture.

After his first four years in Malaysia, Denis praised God for the way the local Christians had begun to shoulder responsibility for evangelism and teaching. He wrote in *The Millions*, 'The Sunday School in Batu Duabelas is staffed by Chinese teachers, who are taken there in a car owned by another Chinese. At the Thursday Bible Study in Langkap a dozen or so working young people gather round the word of God in Mr Lai's shop. In every meeting there are Chinese fellow workers alongside the missionaries and they often take the lead. This is what we have asked you to pray for.'[69]

Some years later, Lai went to Singapore to train for Christian ministry and became an effective evangelist throughout Malaysia.

Foreign workers in other villages up and down the country were having similar experiences as they encouraged local Christians to take the lead. So in spite of clumsy initial attempts and poor language skills, from these tentative beginnings God was starting to form his church

Church buildings

Gradually the work progressed in the south Perak area and the missionaries had the joy of seeing church buildings going up.[70] As early as 1956, a ground-breaking ceremony for a new church in Slim River was held, as the earlier one had been destroyed. Soon the building was completed, and an extension was added in 1974 to accommodate the growing congregation.

In Tapah there was already a Christian cemetery, and about 1962 a beautiful all-purpose church and vicarage were erected in the grounds. Here groups of believers and young people in the district gathered. Youth days and conferences were held there, and many people were built up in their Christian faith. Again, as the work progressed, additions were made to the building.

George Williamson, OMF's first Superintendent for their Anglican work, had been ministering in the Cameron Highlands from 1953 onwards, reaching the British soldiers there. A rest and recreation centre had been set up in the cool of the mountains to provide a break from the tensions and dangers of the Emergency. When the British army moved out in 1960, they gave Williamson a hut for a church building. A retired headmistress called Miss Griffiths-Jones gave some land on which the hut could be erected. This building became the Anglican Church in Tanah Rata, where all visitors and the OMF children of the Chefoo School worshipped.

In 1970, Bishop Roland Koh approved the proposal for a place of worship in Bidor, the first New Village that OMF had entered. Initially the missionaries had stayed in the Red Cross House and held Sunday services in their home. In 1967 they rented an old house at the entrance to Bidor New Village for worship. The Christians soon felt it was time for a permanent building, and in 1971 Reverend David Uttley, who was then in charge of the OMF work in Tapah, drove to Bidor in order to purchase a house that could be used as a church. But a heavy lorry met him head-on along the winding road and he was tragically killed. His death was a terrible shock not only for his wife Barbara, but also for all of his fellow workers. How true it is that the Adversary contests every advance of the gospel. Challenging the evil one in his territory can be very costly indeed.

But the work of God continued, and through sacrificial giving the money was raised to purchase a terrace house as a Gospel Centre in Taman Chit Loong, Bidor. With increased growth and a grant from the diocese, a larger shoplot was bought and beautifully renovated in 1992. St Andrew's Church, Bidor can now hold a hundred people and is the centre for outreach into the nearby towns and villages.[71]

I had the privilege of meeting a veteran worker from this church in 2005.

◆　　　◆　　　◆　　　◆

Reverend Stephen Ng

'What encouraged you to be such a keen evangelist?' I asked Stephen Ng.

'I firmly believe that the gospel is the only way to change human nature – it's the only power that can solve the problems that human sinfulness creates.'

Looking into Stephen's thin face, alight with joy, I could see how Jesus Christ had fully captivated his heart.

Stephen Ng had been a young schoolteacher in Coldstream New Village when he was converted at a Lutheran Youth Camp in 1961. He soon started coming to Betty Meadows and the other OMF missionaries in Bidor, just seven miles away, for teaching. The church in the Red Cross House became his spiritual home as he worshipped with them twice a week.

Hungry to grow as a Christian, he devoured all of the Bible correspondence courses they could offer. 'Upward Path' was the first one. After he completed that, Marion Parsons put him in touch with the distance learning department at London Bible College. He studied hard and worked his way through several of their courses.

At the same time he was sharing his faith at the school where he taught, in spite of the jeers and laughter from others. One of his colleagues saw him giving thanks to God before eating his lunch and said, 'Don't be so crazy, even though you believe in Jesus!'

As a result of his fearless witnessing he was soon given the nickname 'Mr Jesus'.

Undaunted, he borrowed a classroom and started a children's meeting. But the objections came thick and fast. 'Sack him!' people demanded of the headmaster. When he refused to act, someone wrote to the board of governors, and then even to the Minister of Education, complaining that Stephen Ng was using a classroom for Christian meetings.

Stephen refused to be silenced. He rented the upstairs of a wooden shoplot, and 30 to 40 of his schoolchildren crowded in for meetings. It was so warm they could only use it at night. He found it difficult to reach adults and only about ten came in those early days, but many children were touched for God.

In 1974, when because of visa problems there were no more OMF missionaries available, Stephen Ng and his wife moved to the church house in Bidor to supervise the work there, while still keeping an eye on Coldstream. He was able to hand over his children's work in Coldstream to a Christian kindergarten teacher, and he encouraged the adults to come each week and worship with them in the larger centre of Bidor.

Today, it is not only Bidor Church that has a fine building – Charis Church, Coldstream was opened in 2003. Stephen Ng himself had never planned to be ordained, but with the severe shortage of ministers he agreed to pursue ordination in 1994. He spoke very appreciatively of the OMF missionaries. He commented, 'They were the only people willing to carry the gospel to the small villages and towns. Big numbers go to Ipoh, the state capital, but no one else preaches in the villages.'

While listening to his account of his faithful unsalaried work over 43 years, I praised God for raising up dedicated men like Stephen Ng. Stephen actively witnessed for his Lord through difficulties, loneliness and much opposition. He exemplifies for us all what Paul wrote in 2 Corinthians 4:17: 'Our light and momentary troubles are achieving . . . an eternal glory that far outweighs them all. So we fix our eyes not on what is seen, but on what is unseen. For what is seen is temporary, but what is unseen is eternal.[72]

♦   ♦   ♦   ♦

An evaluation of the Anglican approach

'What do you feel now about OMF's pioneer days in the Anglican work?' I asked Denis Lane when I visited him in 2005.

He thought for a moment. 'The mission was facing three problems when they first started work in Malaya,' he replied. 'Firstly, we were a new mission attempting to integrate with a more established work. Naturally there were differences of approach, and sometimes they appeared to look down on us as newcomers. Then, secondly, colonialism had only just ended, and the Anglican Church was automatically linked in people's minds with British rule. So we felt at a definite disadvantage inviting people to join what was seen as a colonial church. And thirdly, as regards the Anglican work, we came as evangelicals into a High Church diocese, where uncertainty reigned initially as to who these newcomers might be. The Diocese of Singapore and Malaya preached the gospel message, but they clothed it with much outward ceremony and tradition which we were not used to.'

'That certainly must have put you at a disadvantage,' I broke in.

'Yes, and what was more: OMF always emphasised evangelizing into unreached areas,' Denis continued. 'Many of us who were not senior missionaries felt that the mission was slow to place workers in the central towns. The trouble with the villages was that once the Emergency was over there was a constant flow from the villages to the towns for education and job opportunities. Because of this, many of our key young people were soon lost to our village churches. In addition, Communist influence remained strong in the villages for many years.'

I could sense the frustration in Denis' voice as he relived the situation.

This emphasis on unreached areas all over the world still hinders the ability of missionaries to grasp opportunities in places where the gospel has begun to gain a foothold. Often it is much more effective to galvanize and train the already evangelized themselves to share the gospel, rather than the foreign worker attempting to do this. The local Christians may be relatively newly converted and inadequately taught, but they know the language and culture and are freshly aware of the amazing change which has taken place in their own lives. So they can gain a more ready audience for the good news of Jesus Christ.

Denis continued with his reminiscences. 'Another problem arose from our placing ordained workers in the villages.'

I was surprised. 'What was wrong with that?'

'You see,' he went on, 'when we left, the national church could not afford to put highly qualified people in such insignificant places. Yet these churches had grown used to having an ordained person and were not willing to have a mere evangelist.' He smiled as he remembered something else. 'Someone commented, by going to the villages OMF was stifling the evangelism of the town churches. They could then see little need to be involved themselves. Sadly we hindered the gospel by this strategy.'

'But we all see things more clearly with hindsight,' I remarked, 'and the strategies of the time were reached by trial and error after considerable struggle.'

'Going back to "the town versus the villages" tug-of-war,' he went on, 'we had some courageous and effective senior missionaries who had laboured in rural areas in China. Their main mission emphasis was on evangelism, and the diocese in which they had worked was fully evangelical. This made them hesitant in Malaysia to work alongside the established town churches, which were not so clearly evangelical. However, new workers who came fresh to Malaysia were used to rubbing shoulders with people who held different views. We began to question the policy of concentrating on village evangelism. We wanted to move into the towns. Towns are more strategic. They are important centres, and can be used to disciple and build up the local Christians. Sadly a strong disagreement developed between the two groups which was not easy to handle.'

'Yes,' I rejoined, 'helping a team of strong-minded, gifted people to work smoothly together calls for great skill in leadership. It also presents a challenge to each individual to be humble enough to listen to other people's points of view.'

Denis reminded me that over the years the field council changed and the newer workers gained influence. He was appointed superintendent after his first home-leave.

John Hewlett, a young and gifted New Zealander, took over from him when Denis and June moved to head-quarters in Singapore. Denis and John had both been keen to make the most of the opportunities in the towns, and so OMFers were appointed in two key centres, Taiping and Penang.

This led to some important relationships forming. For instance, John Hewlett worked alongside and in close friendship with Reverend Choa Heng Sz, the gifted vicar of a Chinese church in Penang. He later became Bishop of Sabah, a friendship that was fruitful for both of them and for the gospel. The Anglican bishop in Kuala Lumpur, the Right Reverend Dr Lim Cheng Ean, served as curate to John Hewlett for a time and they had a good relationship.

Another person who was closely involved with OMF and played a significant part in Anglican ministry was Moses Tay from the Presbyterian church in Muar, Johor. A doctor by profession, Moses moved to Singapore, became a non-stipendiary Anglican minister and eventually the Archbishop of Singapore. Years later he was a leader among Asian and African bishops taking a stand against the appointment of practising homosexuals in prominent positions in North American and British churches. So loyalty to the Lord and to biblical revelation came back from the East to the West, as the younger churches held the mother church to God's standards of Christian truth.

Influence in the Singapore diocese

In the early days, the Diocese of Singapore and Malaya covered the whole country. But when Malaysia was constituted in 1957, two separate dioceses had to be formed.

Several members of the OMF Anglican field served in Singapore. Here Chris Ellison provided a crucial influence. Pastoring an English-speaking congregation in the Queenstown Chinese Church, he had a key evangelistic and teaching ministry at a time when many English-speaking young men were becoming Christians. Several of them had been converted through student ministry in the university. Chris Ellison nurtured and supported many of these young men, and a number of them went into the Anglican ministry – resulting in a large number of evangelically minded clergy. This in turn significantly affected the outlook of the entire diocese.

So the steady work of pastoring and biblical teaching began to yield results. But new government regulations soon began to take their toll. In 1967 the Malaysian government tightened restrictions on foreign visitors. A 'ten-year rule' was established. Very sensibly they argued that foreigners working in their country ought to be able to train nationals to take over from them within ten years. So visas would not be renewed beyond that time. However, they also refused to issue any more missionary visas. Numbers of overseas workers fell drastically after 1967.

Soon there were few missionaries to work even in the larger towns, let alone the smaller villages. Sadly, the OMF leaders were slow to explore alternative methods of entry. Where other missions were already launching into tent making (serving the national church through their professional skills),* OMF directed their new candidates to other countries which were easier to enter. They encouraged only a very few professional workers to be associated with them in the following years.

---

* This practice is called tentmaking after Paul's example in Acts 18:3.

So what happened to the work in those villages in Perak after OMF had to pull out?

◆   ◆   ◆   ◆

Canon Ng Moon Hing

'Our vision is to establish a church in each . . . village. We are targeting ten churches in three years . . . They will probably take a very long time to be self-supporting and self-governing. Our hope is seeing each of these churches as vibrant Christian communities that can be self-propagating, with Christ-centred transformed lives seeking to glorify God and bringing worthwhile blessings to their own villages and eventually the nation.'

So reads the original vision statement of the Anglican Village Ministries set up by the Venerable Canon Ng Moon Hing, Archdeacon of Southern Perak in 1993.

God directs his servants in amazing ways. When Ng Moon Hing was a student at the Seminari Theoloji Malaysia he did a research paper on OMF's Anglican work. Some years later he was led to go on mission trips to Sabah and then India. He was struck by the needs of the many villages in these countries and he was challenged by the unreached small villages on his own doorstep in Malaysia. After writing a paper describing this spiritually needy situation and talking with the bishop, he called for something to be done.

'You start the work,' the bishop told him, 'but you must continue being the parish priest at St Peter's Church, Ipoh as well. I have so few ministers, I can't release you from parish work. But I think you can tackle both jobs.'

At first Moon Hing was reluctant to split his time between two important tasks, but later he came to see what a help the congregation of St Peter's became to the growing work of evangelism in the villages.

Together with Mong, the OMF Malaysia Home Director, I met Canon Ng Moon Hing at St Peter's Church. He had a clear open face, neat dark hair and was casual and relaxed in a bright lime-green Aertex shirt.

'So the villages you are concerned with are the very ones where OMF worked 20 years ago?' I asked him.

'Yes,' he replied. 'But, sadly, practically all the OMF work in the villages has disappeared. I counted up – they had 14 stations, and only Bidor, Slim River and Tapah still have churches.'

I was saddened by this. 'Why do you think that is?' I asked.

'OMF never believed in buying a building, they never invested in property,' was his reply.

I remembered the mission's original strategy not to purchase property because of the uncertainty of how long they might be able to stay. 'Might there have been additional reasons?' I countered.

'There are three main problems in the villages,' he replied. 'Firstly, many of the gifted people move to the towns where employment opportunities are much better. In fact, most of the adults are gone, leaving only the mothers and grandparents to look after the children. Then there's the problem of education. The villages only have primary schools, so the brighter students must go to the towns to continue their education. Some villages have a 50 per cent drop-out after primary school, as it is too costly to send their children to the town. Even if they do go they have to leave by 5 a.m. and don't get back home until after 7 p.m. So the children are exhausted. And then there's the moral situation. Quarrels break out in the crowded houses, foul language is often heard. Drugs are freely available and many become addicted and, what's more, motorcyclists tour the villages with cheap pornographic videos and every home has a video player, no matter how poor they are.'

'Well, it's wonderful you have this vision to reach into such needy areas, and great that someone is picking up the challenge. How have you been going about it?'

'We started in 1993, working closely with The Gospel to the Poor, a para-church church-planting ministry. Together we surveyed the villages to decide which ones to concentrate on, and then we offered tuition as a means of building relationships. At first they were often quite suspicious, but when they saw our sincerity their suspicion melted and we could begin to share the gospel. We are involved in social action too, looking out for needy and poor families. Sometimes we help clean the home, or repair a house, or take sick people to hospital.

'We've divided the villages into two regions,' he went on, 'and we have a full-time evangelist in charge of each region. Teams from St Peter's and other churches also help in evangelism. In 1996, 1997 and 1998 we ran Grass-Root Evangelism Training in Chui-Chak Gospel Centre and Mambang Di-Awan.'

As Reverend Ng continued speaking, I realized I was hearing familiar names from the old days when OMF had been there: Chui Chak, Langkap and Batu Duabelas, where Denis Lane had started evangelism in the 1960s, and Mambang Di-Awan, where Dr Max Gray had begun work in the Red Cross House way back in 1955. These and other names rang bells for me. Yes, it was regrettable that there was little evidence of the earlier work, but apparently some who had been contacted then were now believers. And others had moved on to the larger towns and served in key ministries there.

But the great cause for thanksgiving was that the Malaysian church now keenly felt the challenge of these unresponsive and difficult places. And they are seeing fruit – far more than the missionaries ever saw. The Christians in Mambang Di-Awan now have a lovely building called Shekinah Church. Under Reverend Ng Moon Hing's leadership, within three years they had grown to more than 60 members, and so they have now divided to form another church in nearby Ayer Kuning. Many other villages now have house meetings or a gospel centre linked with the Anglican Village Ministry.

'God's kingdom is spreading – not only among the Chinese,' he went on, 'but also among the Orang Asli, the original tribal people of Malaysia who still largely live in the jungle.'

'That's very encouraging!' I exclaimed. 'I remember visiting an Orang Asli village – the wooden houses were very simple, up on stilts, and there was no running water or sanitation.'

'Yes, many of them feel they have been neglected, and they are so pleased when we come and show an interest in them. We've offered help with goat and chicken rearing. This leads to some income generation and provides them with better nutrition. In some villages we've tried fish farms too. That's a good source of protein when they can catch their own fish. Another project we've tried has been to help someone start a sundries shop. We buy $200 worth of provisions and give this as a gift to start them off. We teach them how to keep accounts and make a profit. It doesn't always work. But if it does, maybe shops can be set up in the villages and the owners will have a steady income.'

It was even more encouraging to hear that Reverend Ng recently started a small Bible school for the Orang Asli in the hope of training up more leaders in the villages.

Reflecting later on our fascinating conversation with the Canon, I commented to Mong, 'You never can tell what work will last. The fruit from OMF's work in this area appears meagre to some. Yet the initial tough task of ploughing and sowing is essential before any reaping can take place.'

'Yes,' she replied, 'the ripening harvest may not come until years later. Each must be content with their own task, whatever the Lord of the harvest commands. His words in John's Gospel are so true: 'One sows and another reaps' (Jn. 4:37).

'But remember too,' I added, 'that many of our converts moved into the towns and threw their weight into the churches there. I'm sure we shall hear more of the impact they made elsewhere.'[73]

7.

Reaching the Multitudes

'We are washing out the topsoil. There isn't so much tin in that. But the deeper we go, the more we shall get.'

Marion Parsons, working in Bidor in the 1950s, was standing on a crazy structure of poles and planks, 50 feet above the ground, when the Chinese overseer made this remark to her.[74] He had been plunging his hand into the swirling mass of slush in the washing ditch in front of them. But he failed to find the traces of tin he was looking for.

It was Marion's first visit to a tin mine. The water from a nearby lake was being pumped through two high-powered hoses which, directed at the hillside, brought the stones and tree stumps and earth crashing down. The mixture was then pumped up to a height of nearly a hundred feet, where it burst out into a great wooden trough and flowed down the sloping beds on the far side. The stones tumbled out through a chute and the tin sank onto the filter beds while the water flowed on to return to the lake.

Standing between earth and sky, with the noise of the flowing slush in her ears, Marion saw the tiny workmen far below as a picture of her team in Bidor. The prayers of her prayer partners were like the mighty jet of water directed at the strongholds of evil around her.

'Yes, the deeper we go, the greater will be the results,' she thought to herself. 'We need patience to continue on and on until the results come at last.'

And she wrote home calling for more urgent prayer, knowing that the weapon of prayer is 'mighty through God to the pulling down of strongholds'. This was the only force that could counteract the huge odds stacked against them.

Prayer: The essential ingredient

OMF always emphasized prayer as being vital to their work. They could see that the local religious beliefs were deeply rooted, and could not be shaken unless some far greater power was called into play. They also knew that they themselves were totally inadequate on their own. Only if God was at work could anyone change people's beliefs. Only by the power of the Holy Spirit could men and women come to acknowledge Jesus Christ as Lord and Saviour.

In the early days of their work, the Anglican team based in Tapah described their fortnightly days of prayer. The road leading to their home saw frequent and varied processions. There were funeral processions – colourful and noisy affairs, accompanied by gaudy banners, large paper houses, cars and even aeroplanes for the use of the departed. The daily procession of rubber-tappers passed every morning at 6 a.m. Chinese women and girls cycled past, protected from poisonous insects and weeds by tight-fitting long-sleeved *sam foo* and brightly coloured headscarves. Heavy military vehicles lumbered through in long lines, part of *Operation*

Chieftain, Tapah district's final effort to starve out or capture the terrorists. And the first and third Thursdays of each month saw a group of missionaries coming down the road, gathering together to pray.

They started at 9 a.m. with a communion service, knowing it would deepen their fellowship and tune their hearts for intercession. From then until 1 p.m. there was a continuous flow of prayer and praise. They prayed for individuals interested in the gospel, for young Christians being tested, for the regular meetings and special youth or evangelistic efforts, for missionaries in their hopes and discouragements, and for those on home assignment. Then they all sat down to a delicious Chinese meal. Tongues were busy as well as chopsticks as all were anxious for news and views on various field matters, while Superintendent George Williamson kept the conversation lively with his sharp humour. George had overall responsibility for leading and developing the ministry, and he worked closely with the local Anglican leadership.

OMF groups everywhere followed a similar pattern, sometimes with monthly and sometimes with fortnightly days of prayer. The mission emphasized their dependence on God and his working in grace in people's lives.

Parable of the jungle

It was not only the tin mines which gave the missionaries parables to think about. A few years later Marion Parsons wrote about a walk through the jungle:

> Immediately out of the bright glare of the noonday sun we were wrapped in darkness. Every tree was festooned with lichens, ferns and creepers, which hung and

dangled around us. The undergrowth was wet and dank
. . . and all the time we felt like intruders . . . We were
infinitesimal . . . in the midst of the mighty growth
around.

The few thatched houses on stilts always seem to be
fighting the jungle growth. You see the housewife
sweeping up leaves and she is like a pygmy pitting her
strength against a giant.

But the jungle can be overcome . . . With infinite patience
clearings have been made by vegetable growers, and
these supply the cities and villages on the plain with
fresh vegetables and flowers . . . The jungle – dark, sinis-
ter, overpowering as it seems – can be cleared.

It often seems that [my] little semi-detached house,
right in the centre of Lawan Kuda, is a tiny clearing in
Satan's jungle. The spiritual hosts of wickedness – Satanic
hatred, moral filth, evil language, and all that pertains to
'people without God and without hope' – surround this
place, press in upon it, and seek to smother us with
unfriendliness, apathy, mockery and blasphemy. Over six
hundred homes in this village . . . *and ours is the only home
where God is worshipped*.

She went on to describe small patches of sunshine,
which were beginning to break through the darkness.
The reading class was one of these, even though hostile
rumours had been spread initially that if you finished
the reading book they would force you to become a
Christian. Fourteen young teenagers who could not
afford schooling were now coming fairly regularly five
nights a week. The lessons Marion taught were based on
a gospel reading book, and by the end of three readers
the pupils were able to read a Gospel for themselves.

Twice a week Marion opened her home for children's
meetings, and 40 youngsters were coming regularly.

Marion commented, 'They are a wild, undisciplined lot, but even a little child can be saved. So we press on.'

She also started a lending library of Christian books in Chinese and English. These went into homes the missionaries could never enter, and were read by people who never bothered to listen to anything they might say.

Another ray of light was Dr Max Gray's visits three days a week. Marion and her team-mates took it in turns to chat with the patients and try to make friends. But the reception was 'cool, calculating and uncooperative'. The little team grasped at the slightest interest shown. One woman confided quietly, 'I pray to Jesus every night, but I haven't time to come and see you.' Another woman whose husband was dying asked anxiously, 'Is it all right if I worship the spirits in the morning, and pray to Jesus at night?'

But all the time the missionaries sensed an underlying current of fear which was like stifling creepers smothering and killing the trees. It pervaded the atmosphere. Everyone was afraid of something. One evening an older girl confided to her friend, 'I'm so afraid. That man died today and his spirit will be out tonight.' It was with great joy that Marion heard Jade Flower, age eleven, reply with confidence, 'You need not be afraid. You ask the Lord Jesus to take care of you!' And she took the older girl over to a poster with a simple prayer: 'Please Lord Jesus pity me, take care of me, take away my sin and save my soul.'

Another smothering creeper proved to be ancestor worship, clinging with its tendrils tightly around their hearts. Marion learnt that if a young daughter were to become a Christian, that would not necessarily generate much hostility. But the sons, particularly the eldest, were expected to continue the ancestor worship. If they became Christians, who would perform the funeral rites for the departed? Were the dead just to be laid in a ditch like dogs, with no rite or ceremony? Throughout their life the deceased would have been paying into some burial society, secure in the knowledge that after their departure they would be duly laid to rest, with priest and gong and sacrificial cock, and mourners in white sackcloth with pall and coffin. Were they to jeopardize all this for a foreign whim? The clinging tendrils of the old religion were strong.

Barbara Hovda in Sungai Chua wrote of a woman who wanted to believe in the Lord, but one thing held her back. She had made a vow to the temple god for the protection of her only son, a lad of twelve. For days she struggled with the matter while the missionaries prayed fervently for her deliverance. At last the bonds were loosed, her heart was opened and she trusted Christ. Next morning, as she came to visit Barbara, she greeted her with the word 'peace'. Her beaming smile glowed with the peace she had found with God and with others.

Evangelistic methods

So what methods were the missionaries using to win people to Christ?

Overcoming suspicion and building friendships were often the initial steps. David Priston, living in Lawan Kuda, described the house to house distribution of tracts, which was the first step for most missionaries as they began their work.[75] Systematically they visited each of the seven hundred homes in that village. David wrote:

> Each double door was pasted with a god looking like a
> devilish king of diamonds. The acrid smell of incense

rose from freshly kindled incense-sticks planted in the red-painted condensed milk tin nailed outside the door. Tattered red and black character scrolls giving the names of deities adhered to the doorways, the whole giving the sight and smell of heathenism.

We come to the first house and peer in. Hens and children scamper in and out as we hand over a tract . . . Few ask us in, and only one or two have shown interest. One cheerful, intelligent woman looked suddenly sad and admitted she had no heart peace. We talked for half an hour . . . (but) the gods are still on her door.

Sometimes people are out, and a bright padlock may hold the frail doors together. We slip the tracts through a crack and pass on, accompanied by the usual crowd of children commenting freely on all we say or do. But the heart-doors are all shut, and hide lives of aimless toil and self-seeking.

David concluded by saying, 'I can hear the sound of guns or bombs this morning. I wonder how long we have got.' During the height of the Emergency the missionaries never knew if they might be forced to leave with only a few days' notice.

He added to his prayer partners, 'It needs your shoulder of prayer to force these doors open and let the Light in.'

Sometimes in the course of handing out tracts the missionaries came across Christians. Betty Meadows, living in Tapah Road, wrote:

We came across her chopping wood outside her home – a little old wrinkled woman, clad in a severe-looking Chinese jacket and trousers. 'Is there anyone in your family who can read?' we asked, producing a tract. The old lady's face lit up with interest. 'Come in and sit down,' she said. We followed her inside, out of the hot sunshine, and sat down on a bench by the door. In the far corner a black pot boiled merrily over a bright fire. And my gaze travelled over the well-swept floor back to our hostess. A faraway look came into her eyes as she listened to Ethel Barkworth speaking. Then she spoke,

'It's fifty-five years ago since I heard about him and I cannot remember much now.'

That was when she had been living in China. As Ethel continued to tell about Jesus, gradually a little group gathered round us listening quietly, two boys and a small girl who twisted her hands shyly when I looked at her . . .

We had to leave at last for there were more homes to be visited. But again and again as we cycled back I thought of this old lady . . . The long years had almost erased from her memory the fact that God had given his Son for her sake. But she knew that there was one true God, and, in spite of the incense sticks which she sold in her shop, [we noticed that] there was no idol shelf in her home.[76]

Prayer for guidance

When Harold and Lucinda Wik went to Rengam in 1952 they were acutely conscious of their lack of experience in pioneer missionary work.[77] They were among the '1948-ers', the group of missionary recruits who had not been able to move into the interior of China. They prayed earnestly to the Lord for guidance as to the right place in which to minister – and guide them he did. A murder outside Rengam prevented them from going to a nearby village for some time. On finally arriving at the village, thirsty after travelling in the tropical heat, they went first to an open-air café. Placing a pile of tracts on the table beside them, they ordered drinks. A middle-aged farmer saw the tracts and came and spoke to Harold and Lucinda. He told them that his grandparents had been Christians in China, and his parents also. Yes, he was a Christian too, and he would be glad to introduce them to the two or three other Christians he knew in the village.

From that first contact a real friendship developed. Mr Tsang was willing to teach them his dialect and he came to visit them in Rengam once a week. He noticed the gospel posters round the wall of their front room, the benches for the little meetings they held there and that the textbook they used most of all was the Bible. During the months the Wiks lived in Rengam he became a reliable fellow worker, and they were sad to say goodbye when they were asked to move to another area.

But two years later, en route for furlough, they visited Mr Tsang again. On the walls of *his* front room there were now gospel posters, and benches for the little meetings *he* held there. In the place where there had been half a dozen isolated Christians, Mr Tsang was now the spiritual leader of 15 or 16 believers. Yes, the seeds of the gospel were beginning to bear fruit despite the hard soil, and the sowers and reapers were now the local Christians.

Witnessing as they travelled

As the danger from the Emergency gradually began to recede, the missionaries were able to travel more from place to place. Grasping every opportunity, they shared their faith wherever they went. David Bentley-Taylor described a train journey he took through Johor State with the coconut palms and rubber trees fringing the line, interspersed with rough wasteland covered with scraggy trees and deep, matted grass.[78]

'Term has just ended and a mob of students poured into the buffet car, shouting, ragging, hooting. It was the university rugger fifteen off for a fortnight's tour of the Federation.' David soon got into conversation with them, listening to their stories and challenging them about the friendship of the world being enmity with God and the necessity for a bold, unashamed Christian life and witness.

In Perak State Ellen Lister and Marion Parsons also often used public transport. Ellen was a gifted artist and made some beautiful paintings of village life. They wrote, 'You have heard of pioneers who tramp through forests, of pioneers who climb high mountains . . . but have you ever heard of pioneers by bus?' And they regaled their prayer partners with stories of what had happened to them,

'After placing my zip-bag full of library books under the bus seat, I settled down to look at my notes. A young Chinese student started up a conversation in English. I found he was a rubber expert speaking several languages.'[79]

Having learnt about his job, Ellen was able to share what her own work was, telling him about Christ.

Travelling in North Perak, over a hundred miles from Tapah, they bussed to Bagan Serai on the bank of an irrigation canal. From there they set off by bus to a different town each day, travelling along straight roads between the irrigation canals. 'As far as the eye could see there were flat flooded rice fields, and the emerald green young rice plants. . . . Men and women . . . worked in mud and water up to the thighs, making a hole in the mud with a pointed stick and pushing in the young plants.'

The two towns in the Selama district which they were interested in were mainly Chaochow speaking. They commented:

> None of us missionaries have learnt Chaochow yet, and there is no such thing as a Chaochow Bible or New Testament. . . . The large districts of Krian and Selama (excepting the towns of Bagan Serai and Parit Buntar) have no Christian workers. So the enemy who sows tares is reaping an abundant harvest. Men and women in these areas are still ignorant of the One who loved them and died for them.

Twice they camped for eight days in a school, exploring the area, chatting to people and giving out Christian literature. Finally two members of their team were led to live in Selama, hoping to reach out to the twelve thousand Chinese in the district. Six different dialects were commonly used in the area, and this complicated their task considerably.

They finished their report saying, 'Why do the *padi* planters sow their seed, plant out the young rice, working in all the discomfort of tropical heat and high humidity? Because they look for a harvest. . . .

'Why does the servant of Christ press on by bus and train, exploring new areas, giving out tracts and preaching the Word? We look for a harvest from the Lord.'

Gospel recordings

The bewildering number of different languages that so many missionaries face gave Joy Ridderhoff from the United States the idea to start a new mission. She travelled to many parts of the world recording Bible stories and evangelistic messages in many different languages and reproduced these on gramophone records. With the multitude of different Chinese dialects in Malaysia, the OMF missionaries were very grateful for the ministry of Gospel Recordings.

Marion Parsons had a bright idea about how to use them:

> The people here are so used to loud radio programmes that [we find that] the Gospel Recordings are invaluable when we use them on the public address system. Believing that things often repeated are more likely to be heard and remembered, we put on the same ninety-minute programme for nine consecutive evenings. They can be heard for about fifty yards each way. 'The entrance of Thy words gives light.' May it be so in this dark jungle.[80]

One wonders whose noise won that day.

A gospel van

Not only did the missionaries use public transport, but a small entry in the May 1954 edition of *The Millions* indicated that the leaders were exploring the possibility of a preaching van to be equipped for open-air work. Within six months it was up and running, with Cecil Gracey in charge and Don Fleming assisting. Cecil was a lively Canadian with a great sense of humour. He was also gifted as a sketch artist. He would hold an audience spellbound as he told a story, and with deft strokes build up a picture on his large easel to illustrate what he was saying.

The small Fordson van was equipped with a public address system, a tape recorder for recording testimonies, a filmstrip projector and screen, Gospel

Recordings in various dialects, a drawing easel and board, a gospel poster and chorus-roll stand and an electric light generator for evening meetings. They planned to travel around the three provinces of Johor, Selangor and Pahang, spending four days in each village where OMF had workers.[81]

'Look, over there's a large tree which should give us some shade,' Don called to Cecil as they entered the village.

'And even better still, it's on a little rise with a ditch in front of it, which might hold the crowds of kids at bay during the meeting,' Cecil replied with a laugh.

'I'll put the generator a few yards over there,' Don continued as the van came to a halt. 'Then it won't be too noisy while you're speaking.'

They both climbed out of the van and got to work. Don placed the loudspeakers on top of the van and connected its long cables to the generator. Cecil got out the Gospel Recordings and, as soon as the records began to play, a crowd of children gathered. A few adults watched from a distance. Cecil's easel was set up on one side of the van and the gospel poster and chorus-scroll stand on the other. The two resident missionaries soon walked over from their house to join them.

After greetings, the small group had a time of prayer followed by a brief discussion planning the programme for the evening.

'We'd better start by making it clear again that we aren't government agents,' Cecil remarked, picking up his piano accordion. 'When the present record ends, I'll lead some singing to get things going and then the meeting can begin.'

In each village they planned a varied programme depending on who was present and which languages were common. In Buloh Kasap, large crowds listened to

Edith Cork speaking on the filmstrip *Pilgrim's Progress*, while another night Minna Allworden spoke using the filmstrip *Crucifixion*. Cecil gave some very effective lightning sketch talks in Mandarin. And a Chinese Christian girl recently converted bravely witnessed in Hokkien.

In Bekok, where there was a Presbyterian church, they enjoyed the help of Pastor Chin, who spoke using various filmstrips. Don, who was still fairly new, gave a message in English, which was interpreted into Mandarin by Mary Welander. Pastor Chin then interpreted what she said into Hokkien. And Cecil spoke in Hakka!

Over six hundred people gathered in front of the Methodist church in Pendamaran to witness the gospel sketched, projected and spoken by Chinese and westerners working together.

After the open-air meeting in Rawang they exhorted a Home Guard sergeant to trust in the Lord. He had been ambushed, wounded and hunted by bandits, and he appeared to realize that *someone* was watching over his life.

In Sungai Chua, Cecil noticed an old granny gossiping the gospel to a group of women. He thrust the microphone into her free hand (the other held a baby), and so Tsai-Nyong suddenly heard her gentle voice amplified many times over. The baby seemed to take exception to this, so Cecil removed the baby while she continued to broadcast. Baby behaved well. Granny wept a little with excitement but quickly recovered and held forth at some length. Tsai-Nyong seemed to have discovered her powers of oratory and gave them unlimited and unending exercise. When Cecil began to wonder how he could bring her to a conclusion without giving offence, the baby started to cry again. So he decided to bring the two negatives together and see if they would make a positive. It worked! Granny said her last few words. Baby gave her last few cries, and the meeting ended happily for all.

To remind us that all this travelling took place in the height of the Emergency, Cecil's account of their first tour ended with the following,

> During these days at Bekok there have been a few ambushes . . . but the good Gospel Van keeps going, bringing the message to the New Villages of Malaya. 'Can anything separate us from the love of Christ? Can danger to life and limb?' (Rom. 8:35, J.B. Phillips)

Some years later, Stanley Rowe took over as the full-time evangelist. Stanley was a tremendous enthusiast, irrepressible and a true inspiration to all. His ministry up and down Malaysia was greatly blessed and many in the New Villages came to Christ through him. For each campaign he was assisted by a fellow missionary whose role it was to drive the Gospel Van, look after all the mechanical aspects including the petrol generator required for the lighting and showing films and slides – and afterwards play innumerable games of chess to help Stanley relax.

Keith Ranger later filled this role, and he remembers frequently being ordered to 'set everything up' to the background of heavy rain crashing down in the nearby jungle and obviously heading his way. He would often finish up soaked to the skin with the meeting cancelled; but there were truly amazing occasions when the rain seemed miraculously to part and pass by the meeting place on both sides, in answer to much prayer and subsequent fervent praise.

Alpha Chang also trained under Stanley Rowe.

◆   ◆   ◆   ◆

Reverend Alpha Chang

Alpha Chang studied at the Malaysian Christian Training Centre in the early 1970s. Part of his training involved learning from OMF missionaries, and he often accompanied Stanley Rowe on his evangelistic trips.

'One day I'd like to take over Stanley Rowe's work,' he thought to himself. 'I couldn't sit in an office like many pastors, preparing their sermons. I want to be out and about, preaching the gospel.'

Alpha Chang was one of the first Christians in the small town of Gopeng, south of Ipoh. He had come to love Christ and devote himself to his service through the work of OMF. He was baptized by Peter Atkins and married by David Uttley, just three days before David's tragic death. Marion Parsons had helped him work through a lay training course, and Fred Collard had asked him to join his preaching team. Fred drew up a big chart covering the local villages, and the team members were sent out each week to a different place. In this way Alpha launched his speaking ministry.

Today he works as a full-time evangelist with the Assemblies of God, travelling all over Malaysia. His wife, who matches her husband's 'Alpha' with the delightful name Omega, also trained with him at MCTC and they form a wonderful team, modelling a husband and wife partnership.

The work in Gopeng had proved very tough for the missionaries. Church growth had been extremely slow and appeared to come to a halt altogether after they had to leave. When Alpha was living there, only 11 Christians gathered for worship week by week. Yet, amazingly, four out of the eleven have now become pastors or evangelists and are having an effective ministry for God today.

The Bible challenges us: 'Who despises the day of small things?' (Zech. 4:10). It might have been easy to feel that it was hardly worth nurturing a group of only 11 Christians. But by the grace of God, his kingdom is being extended through evangelists like Alpha and Omega and the committed members of apparently small and insignificant groups.[82]

8.

Get the Word Out

Evangelism by post

'I wish there were some Bible correspondence course that we could offer,' one missionary was heard to sigh. 'It would be so helpful both for enquirers and for new Christians. We only go to each village once a week, so the interest grows so slowly.'

Letters were written to various centres and, early in 1955, sample copies of a simple Bible correspondence course entitled *The Light of Life* arrived at the mission's headquarters in Kuala Lumpur. It consisted of 24 lessons on John's Gospel. Each lesson contained a brief outline of the subject and some simple questions which could be answered from the passage in the Gospel. The missionaries were delighted to learn that further studies on Mark's Gospel and the book of Acts were in the pipeline.

This appeared to be just what was needed. So, after being checked by the field council, trial copies were distributed to various mission centres in Malaya. The first booklet would be offered free to anyone who was interested, together with a copy of John's Gospel, though the student was asked to contribute towards the postage. If they completed all the questions, a New Testament and a certificate would be given as a reward and encouragement to further Bible study. Both Chinese and simple English versions were available. Many young people in Malaya were keen to learn English and this could be a way of improving their language skills.

Sadly, the immediate response was not very heartening. Most people in villages at that time were too busy just making ends meet to think of doing any study. And many of them had only gone to school for a few years, and that felt long ago. But the missionaries talked enthusiastically about the course to anyone they thought might be interested. Next they placed advertisements in the most popular newspapers and magazines. Posters went up in shops and schools, and wherever possible the correspondence course was advertised enthusiastically in churches and youth groups.

Gradually, a few people tried it and discovered how enjoyable and useful it was. Letters began arriving: 'Please send me more lessons!' one person wrote. Another said, 'I am very pleased that you sent me this course. I now know that I must believe in God and I will be saved from sin.' Four examiners and, later, two assistants were appointed to mark the courses and return them as quickly as possible, to keep up the momentum. So, as *The Light of Life* courses became more widely known, they steadily gained in popularity.

Three years after the course was launched, Emmie Stevens wrote the following:

> Every day the postman delivers a pack of envelopes containing papers for correction, letters, enquiries and gifts from students for postage. Let's open the package and see what they say.
>
> 'Thank you for giving my wife and me the privilege of studying God's precious word. It will help us in our

work for the Master,' from a lay reader and school-teacher.

'But I still do not have peace of heart. Can you help me?'

'I do not understand why Jesus said God had for-saken him. Please explain it to me.'

And, best of all, from time to time we read: 'I want to trust Jesus as my only Lord.'[83]

In this way, lonely Christians in remote villages or rubber estates were being encouraged. Small Bible study groups were being formed. Confirmation classes used it for homework, and many national Christians were built up in their faith.

A Christian bookshop

From the outset of the work in Malaysia, Christian literature was given a high priority.[84] The Christian Witness Press in Hong Kong, supported by OMF, produced a variety of high-quality materials in Chinese. But, as so often happens with literature, the bottleneck was distribution. The missionaries themselves were often too busy to carry much stock. The crying need was for a Christian bookshop.

When they inquired they discovered that a small, locally-sponsored bookshop had already been started in Kuala Lumpur, and the managers were keen for more help. Ken and Vera Price[85] offered to lead the venture, stocking the shop with Christian Witness Press material. They were experienced workers who had been in China and so had fluent Mandarin.

After five years, the ministry of the Evangel Book Centre was flourishing and expanding. But early in 1959 there was consternation: the landlord had served notice to quit. Where might they find new premises?

'You'll get nothing near the centre of the city without key money,'[86] Ken was told. After two months of searching he was tempted to despair. He had visited 40 different premises where key money amounting to tens of thousands of Malay dollars was demanded. It looked as if what he had been told was correct. Large sums of money up front were always expected. Yet Ken knew that OMF had no large stores of money on which he could draw. Every three months, all the money that came in to the mission was distributed for its ongoing work. There were no stocks in reserve.

With only a week to go and still no premises, one Saturday Ken finally found a large room on the first storey of a building right in the centre of the city. Amazingly, no key money was demanded. Quickly he got in touch with the committee, obtained permission to go ahead with the contract, and arranged to sign the agreement. But to his dismay he discovered three unsatisfactory points in the contract, the most serious being that *nothing was to be sold on the premises.*

How could one operate a bookstore without selling books? While it would still be possible to pack and dispatch the many orders that came by post, Ken wanted to display his wares and attract folks in with the hope of reaching many of the local people. Although he was disappointed, Ken had to state that he could not sign the contract.

Ken and Vera talked it over and decided the situation was a challenge to faith and a call to prayer. So they notified as many people as they could, and wonderfully God answered.

On Monday, the other two points were altered satisfactorily. On Tuesday they met with the solicitors again, and after a long discussion the proviso that nothing was to be sold was deleted and the agreement signed. On Wednesday there was bustle indeed. Notices were sent to the press advertising the change of address, and new order forms and stationery printed. Painters took over the whitewashing and painting of walls and ceilings, after carpenters had taken down the old partitions.

The move began on Friday as they shifted the Scripture Gift Mission cupboard and eight or nine huge boxes of literature. But it was a slow business, and there were restrictions for parking lorries in the busy streets. However, many local Christians rallied to help and by nine o'clock that evening the move was complete.

But the miracle lay not only in the provision of the premises, or even in the exact timing and speed of the move, but also in a wonderful transaction which took place. With dust and dirt flying around, carpenters hammering, and removers coming and going, a young lass called Fragrance approached Vera Price. She was spiritually hungry and longed to know the way of salvation. There, in the midst of all the bustle, Vera led her to put her trust in Christ.[87]

The Evangel Book Centre made literature available for all Christians throughout the country. Many missionaries were able to carry a small stock of literature for sale in their own homes more easily. Lending libraries could also be stocked more frequently. For instance, in Alor Gajah, near Malacca, Doris and Al Mace set themselves the target of lending a thousand books for the year. A little child called Chang Fah Chi was surprised and delighted to receive an unexpected gift when she borrowed the thousandth book.

Denis Lane in the Anglican field described a hectic week when Deaconess Emmie Stevens stocked up with several hundredweight of books from the Evangel Book

Centre, and he helped her distribute them. They visited three Chinese-speaking schools, two English-speaking schools and one Tamil-speaking school. With many of the books priced at only ten or twenty cents each, they were pleased to sell over $200 worth of literature. But Denis commented, 'The amount of packing, unpacking, carting, counting, erecting, dismantling, not to mention sweating, involved in such a week is phenomenal.'

As the Apostle Paul reminds us, the missionary task calls for hard work and giving ourselves unstintingly to proclaim the gospel.

Salesman for Christ

Harold Wik, who we met pioneering in Chapter 2, above, developed a new skill to become a salesman for Christ. He was not a natural extrovert like his wife Lucinda, and yet he was burdened to try something different. Knowing that many people would never visit a foreigner's home or even listen from afar at an open-air meeting, Harold was convinced that he must take the literature out to the villages. Loading 150 copies of a Christian magazine called *Dengta* ('Lighthouse') into his ancient Hillman car, he set off for a neighbouring small town. With some fear and trepidation, he worked his way along the main street and visited all the shopkeepers, urging them to buy his attractive magazine. By the end of the day, he had sold 40 copies of *Dengta* as well as some Scripture portions. Curling up to sleep in his car that night, he thanked God for this initial success.

Encouraged by his first trip, Harold repeated the exercise every few weeks. The work entailed long hours going from shop to shop, and it often felt monotonous and draining. But *Dengta* was reaching into areas that had no Christian witness, so he persevered. He travelled extensively to reach nearly two hundred towns, villages and estates. In just a few years he sold over sixteen thousand single copies of *Dengta* and collected 1,700 subscriptions for further copies. He wrote of an 'inner drive' which kept him going long after he might have given up. Those who subscribed to this magazine were finding an attractive introduction to the Christian faith and helpful advice on how to grow as a Christian.

Encouraging writing

Realizing that the impact they were making was still infinitesimal, other outlets were explored. A competition was set up to write a *Tract of the Month*, exploring how literature could be made more relevant. Then Amy MacIntosh started a Christian Writers' Course, encouraging local people to write from their own background and thus reach their peers in a relevant way.

Travelling evangelists

In the 1960s, Keith Ranger took over from Stanley Rowe as the main evangelist. His detailed diary[88] records his speaking and travelling schedule, from Penang in the far north to Johor Bahru down south next to Singapore's causeway. Over the years he gave himself unstintingly to spreading the gospel and building up Christians.

His diary describes vividly the impromptu scene which often took place. For example, in Sungai Chua, the Methodist church building had just been reshaped and the benches were still covered with dust when they arrived and had to be cleaned. Preparing for the film, he suspended a sheet, tying stones in each corner to make it taut. Crowds of noisy children crammed the front rows, and hardly quieted their excited voices as he spoke. Desperately trying to hold the adults' attention, he could see from the corner of his eye that someone was climbing up and down the ladder to the lighting several times. 'Whatever was the matter?' he asked afterwards. 'Oh, it grew far too hot, so we plugged an extra fan in. But then it looked as if the lighting would overheat so we had to go up and unplug it again!' was the reply.

Preaching in such conditions was far from easy.

Yet a substantial increase in the senior Sunday School was reported after this meeting and a number of adult backsliders returned. So he was grateful. But Keith commented that new contacts had to be drawn in 'inch by inch'. It was a ministry that demanded continual perseverance, prayer and a good dose of faith in God's power to accomplish the impossible. Later he found that he was most effective when he returned several times to the same place. Christians had confidence to invite their friends when he returned, since they knew the speaker well.

They often seized the opportunity that local festivals provided. The vivid memory of a Moon Festival evangelistic meeting in Seremban came back to Keith as we reminisced together. The chairs had been arranged in a large circle on the grass and he preached under a bright full moon. Colourful Moon Festival lanterns added to the romance of the scene. All seemed well until he noticed that the microphone was somehow 'live' and not safe to touch. Glancing at the young man in charge, Keith saw that he had bound the tips of all his fingers with insulating tape as a precaution![89]

The Apostle Paul's model for evangelism

The unstinting hard work of the pioneer Apostle Paul set an example for these missionaries. Paul was constantly on the move, preaching in the countryside and in the major cities, in the local markets and in the centres of learning. He took every opportunity to commend his faith whether he was in prison, on a sinking vessel in the midst of a storm, or appearing on trial before kings and governors. Undeterred by any adversity, he could write, 'We are hard pressed on every side, but not crushed; perplexed, but not in despair; persecuted, but not abandoned; struck down, but not destroyed. We always carry around in our body the death of Jesus, so that the life of Jesus may also be revealed in our body' (2 Cor. 4:8–10).

We are all called to follow Paul's example, seen in the ministry of these OMF missionaries, as they used every method they could think of to bring others to faith in Christ. The odds seemed stacked against the spread of the gospel, but foundations were being laid for the tremendous growth of the church which came later by God's grace.

Someone who caught their infectious zeal for evangelism was a young man called Micky Kua, who was brought up in Batu Pahat and was a member of the flourishing English congregation of the Presbyterian church there.

◆   ◆   ◆   ◆

Pastor Micky Kua

'It was from the OMF missionaries that I got my heart for evangelism. I remember them as people who really loved the Lord, and this made them brave enough to

share about Jesus on the streets, open up their Bible picture rolls and give out tracts, with no inhibitions.'
Mong and I had set out to visit Cornerstone Doulos
Church in Petaling Jaya. But I was not prepared for the
sight that met my eyes.

We entered what looked like the door of an ordinary
shop and were shown straight up the stairs. The church
had managed to rent two shoplots, side by side, from the
same owner. Daringly they had knocked down walls to
create a large L-shaped space sufficient to seat two hundred people. The awkward shape could not be helped
because of the stairwell in the centre. But by placing the
platform at the angle of the L, everyone could see the
worship leader and the speaker. The room was set out
with attractive chairs, while band instruments stood
ready on the platform. Power Point equipment and
screens were available, with audio control at the back. In
this simple shop area a very attractive church had been
set up.

The church pastor, Micky Kua, was showing us round
and explaining his vision. Micky was casually dressed,
with greying hair and black-rimmed glasses, and his
manner was lively and warm. He had worked as a college lecturer for many years and was now retired and
giving all his time to this growing church.

'My main interest,' he told us, 'is church planting and
pioneering. So about 12 years ago, with the pastor's blessing, a small group of eight families – just 16 adults and 17
children – were led to start a new church. We are amazed
at what God has done for us. We couldn't get permission
to build a new church, so we met in a terrace house to
begin with. A year later, because our numbers grew so
much, we rented a shoplot. And then when even more
people were drawn in we moved to these two shoplots
here. Church venues are very difficult to get – nowhere is

really legal and neighbours often complain at the singing – so at one time it even happened that our mother church had to move in with us for a while because they lost their venue! But our present situation is great. People find it non-threatening just walking into a shop to come to a church service and we purposely make it very informal.'

'So how do you contact newcomers?' I wondered aloud.

'We think, "How can we meet people's needs?"' he replied. 'We've got some really dedicated church members who don't mind giving up their time. So we started to offer tuition classes in maths and physics for those taking school leaving exams. A good number of young people come to these. And now we've just produced a brochure for English tuition and a Reading Club. That should bring us in touch with more people. We have a church member who works for the AIDS Association and they gave an evening lecture on AIDS and drug awareness. Another one is a lawyer and he spoke on how to write a will, and then a doctor gave advice on health matters.'

'No wonder so many want to come to Cornerstone,' I said. 'You're bursting with ideas on how to reach people. But it must take a while to help them feel part of your church community.'

'That's where the care groups come in,' Micky replied. 'We try to get everyone linked up with a care group where they can really feel at home and ask their questions and grow in the Christian faith. There are seven different care groups with about ten people in each. We train the leaders so they can nurture the others. New members often feel comfortable in a smaller group.'

I looked up at the notice boards and saw a bright sign for a kid's club with some colourful pictures underneath. 'What do you do for the children?' I asked.

'About 40 kids come each Sunday morning – they mostly live in the shops and houses nearby. So friends tell friends and numbers keep growing. We keep encouraging them to bring other children in. And we've some great teachers and helpers who we train, so they're really the best!

'And they lead onto the Youth Fellowship. Saturday afternoon they come and have Bible lessons, discussions and games. We take them to visit an old folks' home nearby so they can learn to help others. And of course the highlight of the year for them is the youth camp, which none of them want to miss.'

'There's so much going on here at Cornerstone. What made you so enthusiastic for spreading the gospel?' I asked.

'We were a young people's church in Batu Pahat when I was a teenager. At that time we didn't have a pastor – the older ones had to encourage the younger ones. But there was an OMF missionary living in a fishing village called Ayam Suloh, six miles away, and we used to cycle over there and help her. Minna Allworden was her name. She asked us to help her give out tracts. I felt apprehensive at first, especially as I couldn't speak Mandarin like Minna could and my Hokkien was only coffee shop talk. So we school kids just prayed and gave out the tracts without saying much. But it was a good learning experience – the first steps in outdoor evangelism.

'When John Edwards from OMF Australia came, we used to laugh at his Hokkien as it was so funny. But two years later his language was excellent and he could preach in it. He used to take us to Ayam Suloh for open-air evangelism as well. I gave my testimony under him in Hokkien, but it was interspersed with English words when I ran out of vocabulary!' Micky laughed.

'Do you feel you gained anything else from the OMF missionaries?' I asked him.

'Thinking back to Malcolm Ryland-Jones and Peter Warner in Batu Pahat in those early days, it was also their stress on Bible teaching. They weren't particularly charismatic speakers, or orators, but they gave us systematic Bible teaching on which to build our lives. They modelled for us how to live out the gospel.

'Mind you,' he chuckled, 'we didn't always click with all of them. One was very English. We used to joke, "here comes the aristocrat!" But he loosened up after some time. And when he visited us years later he fitted in really well.'

'You went on to study at the University of Malaya,' I continued. 'What happened then?'

'I was looking for a church where I could serve,' Micky replied, 'and that's what the missionaries had always said: "Find somewhere where you can get involved!" That's what has led me to focusing on outreach and evangelism.

'After I finished university I noticed how so many Christians my age floundered when they graduated and started work. The University Christian Fellowship gave us all such strong support while we were still studying. But with the pressure of starting a job, and often a new family, people found it hard to integrate into a church. We saw several keen Christians dropping out. So this was another glaring need which I saw needed to be met. So I started the Graduates' Christian Fellowship and led it for ten years, building it up, and then was able to hand it on to someone else.'

'So what has happened to your contemporaries from Batu Pahat?'

'At least eight of them have become full-time Christian workers,' Micky said. 'And of course the congregation now has people of all ages, not just young people like it was with us in the early days. Also in Ayam

Suloh there are now many Christians and they have formed a Chinese-speaking church. In addition, many of us have been praying for our families to come to know Christ. I really thank God that over these 40 years all my siblings have come to believe.'

After spending this inspiring time with Pastor Micky Kua, Mong and I could not help but marvel at the grace of God which changed an ordinary teenager into a visionary pastor of a fast-growing church. He had witnessed this model of a life dedicated to bringing others to Christ many years ago, and now it was bearing fruit in a group of people using every means possible to present the claims of Jesus Christ to their friends, neighbours and relatives. They lived out Paul's instructions to Timothy: 'preach the Word of God. Never lose your sense of urgency, in season or out of season' (2 Tim. 4:2, J.B. Phillips).[90]

9.

The First Fruits

Like a mustard seed

When Annette, Margaret and Fern first arrived in Sungai Way in the early 1950s they prayed for five families to believe in Christ. It seemed an enormous step of faith at the time – three single foreign women, with inadequate grasp of the local language, seeking to change the deeply held beliefs of a community steeped in genera- tions of Buddhism and Taoism. But they held to their prayer target and God honoured their faith.

Sure enough, as the little group wended their way to a nearby pool in a disused tin mine for the baptism serv- ice, five families were represented. There were three couples, a widow and her daughter-in-law, and a woman with six children (her husband had deserted her for a younger woman). Their hearts were lifted in praise to God for the courage of these first believers.

Watching Mr Yong, the father of eight sons and two daughters, being immersed, Fern remembered his earl- ier cry of delight.

'So that's how it was!' he had exclaimed as he fol- lowed in his Bible and listened to Annette telling the

Christmas story and the angel's explanation to Joseph. The baby to be born would be both human and divine and so could act as a mediator between God and human beings.

But their first year had been a hard slog for the three women. In spite of all their efforts, week after week nobody joined them for their Sunday worship. Fern later commented, 'We nearly wore out the Gospel Recording, listening to "He giveth more grace" as we spurred ourselves to keep going.'

But Fern's nursing training was helping them gradually to overcome their neighbours' initial hostility and suspicion. Fern kept a small box of medicines and dressings in the corner of their front room. As her skills became known, a few patients grew bold enough to step inside and consult her. While Fern treated the patients, Margaret or Annette told gospel stories and explained the way of salvation.

One lad who had cut his heel came back many times after it was healed just to hear the stories. Eventually God's love drew this lad to Christ. Another man later testified that he really praised God that he had contracted TB, because it was TB that brought him to the clinic and so to know Christ.

Checking on their patients' recovery gave them entrance into local homes. And little expressions of gratitude began to come their way: a gift of eggs, some fresh vegetables and one day even a live duck!

After a full year's hard work, a turning point came when Paul Contento, an individualistic pioneer and an exceedingly gifted OMF evangelist and Bible teacher, brought a team of four students from Singapore Bible College to run an evangelistic campaign.

'That's amazing. Here are some *Chinese* people who follow this strange religion!' exclaimed the neighbours as they listened to the students preaching in their own dialect. 'Maybe the Christian faith is not just for foreigners after all.'

Mr Yap, the ladies' language teacher, took the bold step of being the first to accept Jesus as his Saviour. In their language study together they had worked their way through one of the Gospels. As he came face to face with Christ, the beauty of his life and the reason for his coming, Mr Yap was convinced that this was the truth. He and a few other curious people began attending the Sunday evening[91] worship service, and so the numbers at last began to grow.

From the beginning the children's work showed the most promise, though numbers were always unpredictable. Fern wrote telling me of her first effort at Sunday School teaching:

> I sweated, literally and metaphorically, over the lesson with my language teacher, trying to get every phrase correct. Feeling very nervous, I launched into my talk, and then was horrified to discover I had run out of material after only five minutes! Not only that, but my audience who had comfortably filled the room suddenly vanished. They wanted to watch a funeral passing by. Only one old granny who had brought her grandchildren remained:

Later on young people's groups were started. Camps at the seaside, where many youths from the various mission centres gathered, developed this mission even further. Chinese pastors from Kuala Lumpur were often asked to speak. Numbers of young people came to faith under their excellent Bible teaching and found greater courage to witness for Christ. Excitedly they realized that there were growing numbers of Christians like themselves throughout their country. This wider fellowship proved a real encouragement to them.

The services held in Sungai Way were very simple, with Scripture readings and a message, interspersed with prayers and hymns. Their aim was not to found a church of a particular denomination but to leave the Christians free to remain independent or to choose a group to join when they had later grown in maturity.

Once a month they invited a speaker, Chinese or western, to conduct a communion service. Fern remembers with some amusement when leading this service fell to her. The bread and wine had been laid out in advance on their rough wooden table. To her horror, although her message was fairly brief, when they came to receive communion red ants had begun to crawl over the little paper cups!

'Whatever shall I do?' she thought anxiously. Turning the tray round so that the least affected cups were nearest to the participants, she prayed hard that no one would notice the scurrying dark specks. Nobody batted an eyelid as they drank, and she presumed she had carried off the situation rather well.

One of the young ladies then remarked, 'Those ants are quite bitter, aren't they?'

Apparently she had not been entirely successful!

Some time later, three older men who had been baptized with Mr Yong's son were appointed deacons and began to take more responsibility in the church.

Challenges for the new believers

Naturally the new Christians faced a number of dilemmas as they attempted to free themselves from their old beliefs and customs. Often, for example, food cooked in the home was placed briefly on the god-shelf before being brought to the family table.

'Is it permissible for Christians to eat such food?' the missionaries were asked. So out came the Bibles, and passages referring to idols and spirits were consulted. God's revelation on Mount Sinai made it clear that he alone was to be worshipped and no Christian must have anything to do with idols or spirits. It was clear that worship of ancestral spirits was not acceptable.

They also discussed passages in the New Testament such as the following: 'an idol is nothing at all . . . there is no God but one. . . but not everyone knows this. Some people are still so accustomed to idols that when they eat such food they think of it as having been sacrificed to idols, and since their conscience is weak they are defiled' (1 Cor. 8:4, 7).

'Yes,' one of the new Christians affirmed, 'my mother is deeply religious, and all the dishes that she cooks have to be placed on the god-shelf. She really believes in the power of those spirits!'

'And that's why the passage continues with a warning,' the older Christian explained. '"Be careful . . . that the exercise of your freedom does not become a stumbling block to the weak." And Paul concludes, "if what I eat causes my brother to sin, I will never eat meat again."'

'That settles it for me then,' this particular new believer decided. 'I can't eat any of that food.'

But other Christians felt that, since the Bible says that 'an idol is nothing at all', they were free to eat everything. They spoke up strongly for their point of view. In such issues that were open to interpretation, the missionaries encouraged church members to look at all the relevant passages and work out for themselves what the Bible taught for each tricky situation.

Basically, all of the Christians wanted to make a clear stand against anything to do with idols and evil spirits.

This could be costly if they were the only Christian in a family. So many a young person willingly ate only rice and ketchup until their parents relented and put some meat and vegetables aside for them.

Mrs Yap, the teacher's wife, confided her relief at not having to make offerings to idols. She had long been haunted by an awful thought: 'How can I ever be sure I've offered enough?' How deeply satisfying it was to know that Jesus had provided a full and perfect sacrifice for the sins of the whole world. There was nothing more that she needed to do except thank him from a full heart and live to bring him joy.

'But what about ancestor worship?' someone else asked Fern. 'We can't forget our ancestors. Everyone must show their respects to them.'

'Respect is one thing,' Fern told them, 'but worship is another. As Christians we must show respect. See what the Ten Commandments say about honouring our father and mother in Exodus 20.'

'But how can we respect them without worshipping them?' This new believer was genuinely puzzled.

'Well, what do you think?'

'I suppose by remembering and talking about the good things they have done,' was the hesitant reply.

'Yes, and keeping their graves tidy,' Fern replied. 'Where there is a choice, it is better to visit the grave at some other time to show respect. If we have to visit during the feast of the Hungry Ghosts,* we can show respect by placing flowers and not participating in the customary religious practices.'

'And remember that we don't need to be afraid of these so-called ghosts,' Fern continued. 'The Bible shows us that God is greater than any evil spirit. Other people

---

* See glossary.

may be afraid, but we have the Holy Spirit and he lives in us.'

Mr Yap, their first convert, had a traumatic experience that tested these confident words. When he heard Mr Yap On Tham (no relation of his) preach on one occasion, he was convinced that he needed to seek forgiveness from his younger brother. It is very difficult in Chinese culture for an older brother to apologize to a younger brother, and apparently Mr Yap struggled over this. Whether it was disobedience to the Holy Spirit, or an attack of the evil one against the first convert, or something else entirely, nobody knows. But, tragically, Mr Yap temporarily appeared to lose his mind. He described it later as feeling as though he was being dragged down into a deep pit. The darkness and helplessness were overwhelming.

Over the following two weeks Fern and her fellow workers were called many times, day and night, to go to him and pray, or sing and read Scripture. But his strange behaviour continued. Then Mr Yap developed measles and, as measles can be very severe in an adult, he was put into an isolation ward in hospital.

While he was in hospital, a terrific electric storm one night terrified him so much that he ran outside in his pyjamas and got soaked to the skin. He was petrified and struggling, and it took six men to carry him back inside again. The hospital wanted to send him to a mental hospital, and the relatives urged his wife to consult the spirits and turn back to idolatry. As soon as Fern heard about it, she hurried to his bedside and managed to persuade the doctor, who amazingly was a Christian, that this was a spiritual and not a mental attack.

Prayer and dogged faith finally brought him through. Groping blindly in the darkness of his deep pit, Mr Yap at last felt he saw a rope. He grasped it and clung on in faith until he felt rescued. Later he explained that he knew this rope was the fact that 'the blood of Jesus Christ cleanses us from all sin'. He kept repeating these words again and again.

Regardless of what lay behind these struggles, Mr Yap emerged a much stronger Christian. He led the church after the missionaries left some years later until his death from cancer in the 1970s. This sort of wrestling with spiritual powers was not uncommon in Malaysia at that time when idolatry was so strong.

Every Chinese child was dedicated to a spirit or deity at the Buddhist temple, so Christian conversion always necessitated not only turning from sin, but also asserting a clean break from the lordship of evil spirits.

Building their own church

As the group of Chinese Christians in Sungai Way grew more confident, they became too numerous to fit comfortably in the missionaries' front room. 'We must have a building of our own,' they said. When the New Village had initially been formed the British government had promised that a site could be made available for a church. But when the residents requested it, the government disappointed them repeatedly. A couple of promising sites, which they had hoped for, fell through. And when at last a plot was granted, it turned out to be the village dump on the side of a ravine.

Having waited so long, the little group of Christians decided to go ahead in faith on this unlikely site. There was a small embankment next to the ravine, and they shovelled hard to toss the embankment soil into the gaping hole. However, levelling the bank still left a large amount of empty ravine. They enquired about buying earth and estimated that they would need at least 50 lorry loads which, at $10 per load, would use up half their building fund before they even started on the building.

Driven back to prayer yet once more, they wondered what could be done.

But, as we have seen repeatedly, God knows our needs long before we ask. At that time the new highway linking Kuala Lumpur to the west coast was being built. And, just when they needed many loads of earth, the road reached Sungai Way.

'Would some of the earth being excavated from the hills you are tunnelling through be available for our building project?' they enquired.

Yes, they were told. That would be possible if a letter was sent promising that the earth would not be sold, since it was government property.

The letter was produced and, in a few days, lorry loads of earth began arriving at the site. All the Christians were mobilized to get the earth tipped into the ravine before the next load came. In the end, nearly 120 loads of earth were delivered, and the only cost was a perpetual supply of soft drinks for the drivers! Fern had a chuckle to herself at God's sense of humour, because her Bible reading from Weymouth's translation the final morning contained the promise that 'every ravine shall be filled up' (Is. 40:4).[92]

How they rejoiced when the church building was dedicated in August 1958, six years after the missionaries first arrived in Sungai Way. The membership had grown to nearly 50, and two dedicated Chinese elders now led them. Later that year the missionaries were able to move on to meet other needs. The church decided not to join any denomination but to remain independent.

Fern later went back to Sungai Way to see the progress and witness the harvest. She wrote me a long letter describing her joy at the reunion.

♦   ♦   ♦   ♦

Updating the story

The little church in Sungai Way has not always found life to be plain sailing. For a few years OMF was able to send other missionaries to help them occasionally, but in the 1970s foreign visas were being refused. At the same time the two church elders were becoming more frail and had less energy, so numbers decreased significantly. Sending an SOS to OMF headquarters, the director suggested they look for help from the nearby Brethren Life Chapel. For two years these fellow Christians generously sent teachers and preachers for the Sunday services, training some local Christians to be able to take over the leadership. Then Life Chapel developed their own problems. But by that time younger leaders in Sungai Way were ready to take over.

Through all their ups and downs, Sungai Way Christian Church has now become fully established. By God's grace they have raised the money to build an even larger two-storey building with an air-conditioned auditorium sufficient for 200 people, and an annexe for the Sunday School. This building was completed in 1988.

The upper floor contains a hall with a capacity for 50 persons together with a library room. There is also a separate section comprising a two-bedroom apartment for the pastor. At the moment the church is in the process of acquiring another piece of land (7,000 square feet) immediately behind the existing building, ready for future expansion.

The Christmas Day service, which Fern attended in 1995, had a full house with vibrant music ministry led by enthusiastic and talented young people. An English congregation has also developed, which was started by Harold Wik and later supported by the Brethren Life Chapel.

Fern wrote of meeting one fine young man who was working full-time in student ministry with the Fellowship of Evangelical Students. How vividly she remembered his father and twin uncle as little boys in her Sunday School. His uncle, Yong Toong Chor, became an elder in the church. He had been one of the earliest graduates of the Christian Training Centre started by OMF in Rawang.

Sundays at Sungai Way Church are very busy, with the English service running from 8 – 10 a.m., the Chinese service from 10 – 12.30 p.m. and an Indonesian service after lunch. More recently, to meet the overwhelming response, the Indonesian church has started another service in the evening. These Indonesians have come as migrant labour to satisfy the shortage of workers in various industries in Malaysia.

Some 150 Sunday School children, as well as the youth, make full use of the upstairs space and the annexe each weekend. Classes are held separately in English and Chinese. Apparently non-Christian parents are very willing to send their children to the Sunday School because they notice that the church children are much better behaved.

In 2005 the English assembly began offering English tuition as a means of bringing more children to Sunday School. A suitable room has been rented from the neighbour next door. The response has been overwhelming, but sadly the class can accommodate a maximum of 45 children.

A recent addition has been work among Nepali migrant workers, and 15 men have been befriended. Fortunately they understand sufficient Malay to be able to communicate with the church workers. And so the church has begun to minister not only in English and Chinese, but also in Malay. The church prays that the Nepali migrant workers will later take the good news back to their home country.

Looking back on this amazing growth from such inauspicious beginnings, one can only praise God for the miracles that he still works today. With variations on a similar theme, these miracles have been multiplied all over the country. Little tigers are indeed becoming bigger tigers.

10.

The Beginning of Training

Poultry, produce and preachers

'How can I be better equipped to serve the Lord Jesus?' Chang To Chia (Dorcas) asked the missionary couple working in her New Village, Karak.

They hesitated, wondering how to reply.

'Well, how did you train?' she persisted. 'What did you have to do?'

'In our country there are Bible colleges, and we could go there to study and learn how to minister.'

'But here in Malaya we don't have a Bible college,' Dorcas replied. 'Couldn't someone start one? There is so much I want to learn.'

When David Day, the new OMF superintendent for the southern part of Malaya, heard about Dorcas' deep longing, he began to pray and to plan. Maybe they could do something, but he would need a Chinese colleague to make this vision happen. Who did he think of? Mr Yap On Tham immediately came to mind.

Pastor Yap, who was in his mid-thirties, was already making a name for himself in the 1950s as a leading Christian and Bible teacher. He was born in China into a

Christian family (his father had been the principal of a London Missionary Society school in Amoy). The family had escaped to Singapore when Japan invaded China in 1937. Twice the young Yap had been challenged by the dynamic Chinese evangelist John Sung's preaching: initially to give his life to Christ when he was sixteen, and then when he was twenty to full consecration to God.

With Japan's invasion of Singapore, Mr Yap found himself spending his honeymoon hiding in the jungle. He had a deep longing to equip himself better for preaching the gospel, and so Mr Yap was the first student to register when the Singapore Bible College was set up after the war. Unfortunately, family responsibilities and ill health prevented him from completing the course. Deeply disappointed, the Yap family moved to the Cameron Highlands where Mr Yap had been given a teaching post. Despondently, he presumed he must give up all ideas of full-time service for God.

But through this time of testing God was preparing Yap On Tham for fruitful ministry. Some years later, when he was transferred to Kuala Lumpur, he met OMF missionaries and asked what he could do to help. A partnership in service was struck up, and Mr Yap often called himself an 'OMF fellow worker'. The OMF leader recalls with chagrin how slow he was to recognize Mr Yap's gifts. The first time they worked together he merely used Mr Yap as his interpreter. It is too easy for the western missionary to assume superiority. They were soon working side by side as equals, however, sharing the preaching and teaching. Yap On Tham started his own church in Kuala Lumpur and was often invited to preach in the villages where OMF worked and to take their baptisms.

He readily agreed to David Day's plans to start evening Bible classes in Kuala Lumpur. A committee was formed, a bank account started and a room hired for two evenings a week. Dorcas and her widowed mother were so keen to attend that they sold their home in Karak and moved the 60 miles to Kuala Lumpur. She took a job as a domestic servant to support the two of them while attending the Bible School in the evening.

Others made equally great sacrifices in order to take the course. David Wong from Kuala Kubu Bharu found work as a school caretaker seven miles from the classes and cycled a total of 14 miles each evening to get there. Andrew Yong of Serdang also was keen to learn. He worked tapping rubber on his father's estate, rising at 5 a.m. every morning. After a hard day's work he showered, had his meal and then cycled 11 miles to the class and 11 miles home again after 9 p.m.

This costly lifestyle took its toll. 'The students are exhausted after a day's work and all this travel, and they are far too tired to study in the evening,' David commented. 'We must think of a new plan.'

'Well, what about a residential training centre?' Yap On Tham replied. 'Suppose the students went out to work to support themselves during the day. Then if they came home to a Christian environment and were on the spot for evening classes, that would lighten their load.'

It would not be easy to find a suitable place within their means, but the two friends felt inspired to pray hard and begin looking. Again, they were reminded that God's clock kept perfect time. A friendly Christian businessman mentioned suitable premises near Rawang, 18 miles from Kuala Lumpur. Surrounded by five acres of land, it held a large red-roofed shady bungalow, once the home of the estate manager, and various smaller offices. This appeared to be exactly what they were looking for. And, even better, the manager of the adjacent rubber estate agreed to employ the students as rubber-tappers so they could earn their living.

The board of the original Bible School took responsibility for the new training centre, with Pastor Yap as its chairman, while OMF agreed to pay the rent and the salaries of the staff. So, from the beginning, Rawang Christian Training Centre (known as Rawang CTC) was a joint Asian-Western venture.

There was much to be done to repair the house and to adapt it for use as a college, and here the different gifts of some of the missionaries began to shine. George Tarrant, who had never expected to use his building skills, found himself overseeing the alterations. And Harold Wik, who had a B.Sc. in agriculture and animal husbandry, enjoyed getting his hands dirty once more, putting up poultry runs and erecting fences for livestock. They planted 250 trees, mostly banana and papaya, as well as some lime and mandarin orange trees. Between his distributing trips selling *Dengta* magazine and other Christian literature, Harold kept an eye on the farm as it developed.

Just at that time Percy and Amy Bromley, who had been teaching in a Bible school in China, were free to come and direct the school. Edith Cork, an exceptionally gifted Bible teacher who became much loved by all the students, joined them. She gave herself unstintingly to befriend and counsel them in spite of her own poor health.

The day in May 1961 dawned when Rawang CTC was to open, but, disappointingly, only two students turned up. The others had run into one difficulty after another. Within a few days, however, numbers had increased to five, and later they settled down at roughly ten or twelve. 'Even our Lord chose only twelve students,' they agreed, 'and look what a mighty work sprang from those twelve disciples.'

However, work on the nearby rubber estate was not ideal. 'I'm so exhausted from rubber tapping,' the students were often heard to sigh. 'It's such an early start to the day, and the money we get hardly pays for our food, let alone anything else!' The teachers saw their tired faces and agreed that after rubber tapping the students had little strength left for study. As the farm developed, it began to provide a steady source of income. They just had to pull together and determine to weather the early days. Soon they were collecting 50 eggs a day from the chickens, the piglets were fattening and the banana and papaya trees producing fruit.

'What's the word in Hakka (or Hokkien or Cantonese) for that expression you just used?' was a frequent puzzled remark during classes. For village people used to chattering in their own language and with only a few years of education, studying in Mandarin Chinese was a big hurdle. But Mandarin was the only language that could bridge their differences, and it was the language of education. So each student tackled it with courage and perseverance. As far as possible the syllabus attempted to cover a normal Bible college curriculum of biblical, historical and theological studies, though at a basic level. Living together in community also provided many opportunities for character building.

To gain practical experience of Christian ministry the students learned how to teach Sunday School, go visiting and speak at open-air meetings. They also led their own young people's meeting each week and took their turn at leading college prayers.

With all this outreach from the training centre it was disappointing to hear Percy Bromley's later comment: 'During my two years leading Rawang CTC we had no fruit at all from the students' evangelism in the surrounding villages.' Hearts were hard and superstition deeply entrenched. The need for perseverance in faith remained great. The rich harvest, which would later develop, had still not begun to ripen.

Percy also later regretted that the training centre did not work closely with the small church in Rawang. The theory was that the CTC students might swamp the local Christians, depriving them of opportunities to develop their own gifts. Rigid separation of 'church and college' was the mindset of the time, whereas they might well have enriched each other.

Before Rawang CTC became well known, they often struggled to make financial ends meet. One year they closed the accounts with only four cents to spare. But over and over again they proved God's faithfulness in providing for their needs. And these needs were increasingly met by generous gifts from local Christians.

A variety of OMF missionaries taught at Rawang CTC. When David and Phyllis Day led the work for several years, Phyllis developed jam and chutney production in the old wine cellar of the bungalow, which produced further funds. 'CTC is the ideal way for training Christian workers,' Phyllis commented shrewdly. 'Farm work shows up the real character of the students. This is key for future pastors. If you can't look after the animals, you haven't yet developed the gifts to look after people.'

A painful dilemma

But Phyllis was also struggling with a heart-rending issue faced by many missionaries at that time. What was the best way to care for and educate their children?

Many of the mission's workers lived in remote areas where the standard of local schooling left much to be desired. Also, although missionary children often were fluent in the local language, it was important that they should be educated in English so they would be able to fit into their home country in later years. Today home schooling is often practised, but it was little known in those days and very little course material had been developed.

The common practice at that time was to send children to boarding school. But herein lay the agony. Little children, no more than six or seven years old, must then be separated from their parents. Twice a year they could return home for a couple of months, but then they must face four months apart from their families, living and studying in the boarding school.

A delightful complex in the cool of the Cameron Highlands was purchased with special gifts to the mission, and this was developed into a well-organized boarding school for primary school children.[93] But many a parent's heart ached at the separation, even though they knew that dedicated and well-trained teachers ran the school, and 'dorm aunties' would care for their offspring after lessons, acting as surrogate parents. Half-term breaks, when parents could stay in the holiday bungalow and visit their children, helped a little to ease the sharp longings.

Everything possible was done to meet the children's spiritual and emotional needs, and after a while the very large majority settled happily into the routine,[94] although nothing could really replace home life within the family.

When children reached secondary school age the separations proved to be even longer. Boarding school in the home country was arranged, with loving and dedicated hostel parents to care for the growing youngsters.

Recently Phyllis wrote to me, honestly sharing the depth of her feelings as a mother:[95]

> When Joy, my last, went off to Chefoo [School] in the Cameron Highlands I felt totally bereft. That was 1963. I

wrote then, 'As individuals we can respond with whole-hearted devotion to Christ's call. But when that devotion of ours touches our *family* and involves them in pain and trouble, that is when the real test comes. That touches the quick. New meanings come into what were slick ideas of discipleship. We tremble before Jesus' stern words to take up our cross. Tears and pain mingle with our once so-bold expressions of devotion to him. The cross bites hard . . .

In 1967 when we returned [to Malaysia] leaving all three at home, David had to complete his studies [at the London Bible College] so I went ahead on my own with the luggage on a freighter, taking five weeks to get to Malaysia. No wonder I got a bit weepy. During the trip I wrote this poem, thinking about the short time we had been allowed together.

For ten months mine!
To see, to touch, to know,
    to have that treasured time in which to grow as
        one;
To share your fun, your joys and fears,
To hear your lively tales of three long years,
To have you with me helping with the chores,
    and go on country rambles out of doors.

How rich these months at home have been to me,
    my lively, lovely, charming darlings three!
The bursts of boisterous fun, the sudden tear,
The warming hug, the evening time of prayer,
The luscious goodnight kiss,
    the soft young cheek,
        can only be enjoyed when loved ones meet.

But now the seas have severed you and me,
Your sweet young faces now not mine to see,

Your voices, once familiar, heard no more,
Your pictures hang so silent on the wall!
   But oh! for you –
      your warmth, your life, your love,
         the human comfort of your flesh and blood!

Yet weakly, Lord, I *can* say 'more than these',
   I love you more,
      though trembling on my knees.
My God, this ointment rare I gladly pour
    on Jesus' wounded feet – and in it all we each shall learn
      through seeming loss and pain
         that God's will done with joy is so much gain.

The letter continues, 'Later when our three came out to
Malaysia for the summer holidays in 1969, the parting
was so painful [for Phyllis' daughter Joy] that she decided the only way to cope was to shut out her feelings
altogether. And that's what she did – thankfully, not for
long.'

Joy later told Phyllis: 'The pain of loving you was too
much to bear when you left me, so I killed it by stopping
loving you. It cost too much . . . You've got to die inside
in order to carry on.'

But Phyllis was able to conclude her letter by saying,
'The Lord has done a lot of healing, and my children and
I are good friends, especially Joy, who is very close to
me.' Graciously God has now arranged that all three of
her children live within 15 miles of her home and they
feel very close as a family. Even though she is now a
widow she is grateful for the way God has brought her
and her family through all the sacrifices.

With prophetic realism the psalmist promises us that
'Those who sow in tears shall reap with songs of joy' (Ps.
126:5). The tears and the pain of countless missionary

parents have eventually brought forth a rich harvest. No sacrifice for God is ever wasted.

And the Rawang team had the joy of watching many of their students move into fruitful ministry. A good number of them returned to their own villages and became humble but valuable church workers. Of the first two students to graduate, Chang Chih Ch'ing went back to Triang, his own village, and served alongside the missionaries there. Dorcas (Chang To Chia) put her training to good use and eventually married one of the lecturers at Singapore Bible College.

Many other CTC graduates moved into key positions of leadership. Wong Kim Sui from Serdang became pastor of a church in Kuala Lumpur which itself spawned daughter churches. He developed a valuable teaching ministry into mainland China. Chang Ch'ui Chen married Huang Fu Ts'ai (both CTC graduates) and together they pastored Sungai Way church for many years before retiring. Lieow Meng Kwang and Mary have been involved in pioneering work among the Orang Asli for many years, supported by various Malaysian churches. And James and Mei Choo Lai recently visited Phyllis Day when their international ministry brought them to England. Phyllis also fondly remembers Catherine Chew and Cheong Wu Mei, two single ladies, who both made a valuable and lasting contribution to Malaysian Care, an indigenous Christian ministry with a vital work among the underprivileged. Further research could reveal countless others who trained at Rawang CTC and gave their lives to serve their Lord and Saviour.

Christ never promised his disciples a bed of roses, but he did promise to build his church. And through the suffering and sacrificial lives of his servants the church in Malaysia is growing.

♦   ♦   ♦   ♦

A visit to Rawang Church

A little deputation of church members was waiting in the small church in Rawang for Mong, K C and myself. Each one had a story to tell of God's goodness to them in spite of many difficulties and much suffering. It was humbling to listen to the way God had led them as Mong translated their stories from the Chinese dialects for me.

Mrs Ooi Bok Lean told us that she had worked as Fern Blair's house help and felt she owed much to Fern's love and care, as she had never known love in her childhood. Fern's Bible teaching had also built her up in her Christian faith. Hers had not been an easy life. When she was only a little girl of nine years of age she had to leave school and look after her younger brothers and sisters. They were desperately poor and life was a constant struggle of cooking, cleaning and laundry.

The years went by and she heard of the Christian Training Centre being set up on an estate near Rawang. By now Bok Lean was sixteen years old. One day Mary Wilson, who had joined the teaching staff, saw her and invited her to come to the youth fellowship. Far too shy to say anything, Bok Lean shook her head. But Mary persisted and some time later, at the third invitation, Bok Lean plucked up courage to go. To her delight she found friends there of her own age and it was a relief to forget her family responsibilities for a while.

Her grandmother, however, was furious when she discovered where Bok Lean had been.

'Who's going to look after your brothers and sisters?' she demanded. 'With your mother away working and only home once a week, I'm not going to do it!'

But Bok Lean was drawn by the love of the little Christian group. Not wanting to miss a gathering, she did all her housework before she left each week. Under Mary Wilson's guidance she trusted the Lord that year, 1969, and then Henry Guinness baptized her three years later when her family at last relented and gave her permission.

Bok Lean has now been married 28 years and lives in Ulu Yam, a few miles from Rawang. When the missionaries had to withdraw from the country, the church met in her home for many years. They now have their own pastor in Ulu Yam and about 70 attend the services. A distant relation of Bok Lean's husband is one of the leaders, and her youngest daughter runs the Sunday School.

Mah See Hong, sitting in his wheelchair, also told of great difficulties. He had contracted polio when still a child and this had cut him off from many people. But when he was twelve years old, in 1966, a group of Christian young people offered to push him up the steep hill to the Rawang CTC for their youth meetings. While he only went a few times, he never forgot the kindness of these young people or the love and care of the missionaries. His polio had always made him feel like an outsider, but when he heard the missionaries preaching in town he sat listening on the edge of the crowd. When he was in his twenties his brother urged him to become a Christian, but something inside him always held him back. At last, when he was thirty-one years old and sitting at the back of a prayer meeting, he felt the Lord touching him and God's love being poured into him, warming him and healing him.

Mah See Hong is still in his wheelchair, but he feels like a different person. He developed a great zeal for the Lord in evangelism and discipling. Now he works in the handicapped centre as a volunteer, sharing God's love with all who come.

Teh Ah Mu is part of the present leadership team of Rawang Church. When he first came to know the Lord there were only ten Christians in Rawang. Now he praises God that there are a hundred. As a child he had a long walk to school and had to pass a stream. He confided in us that, strangely, he often thought about death and wished he could be like the flowing stream, which went on and on. When he was thirteen years old he was invited to Sunday School and went with a few friends.

'Christianity is only for westerners,' his father had exclaimed as he beat him again and again. 'I forbid you to go near them.' Understandably afraid of the pressure from home, Ah Mu kept away. But the missionaries used to meet him in other places and encourage him to persevere.

Sensing something constantly drawing him back, he thanked God that his father's opposition decreased over the years. When he was eighteen and listening to the Rawang students preaching at an open-air evangelistic meeting, he decided to follow Christ. This was a bold step as he knew his father would still not approve. It was a full year before his father would give permission for him to be baptized, as he was the first Christian in the family. Like so many other teenage Christians in Malaysia, he determined to win his family over by his good behaviour and loyalty, and they began to notice how he had changed.

Some years later his father was taken ill. He couldn't sleep but would just sit at the kitchen table with his head on his hands. Ah Mu saw his distress and felt compelled to share the gospel with him. He also took him to hospital and cared for him day and night. Eventually, knowing his father was too ill to speak, Ah Mu asked him, 'If you wish to receive Jesus Christ as your Saviour please just nod your head.' And to his joy his father nodded. He died shortly afterwards, but Ah Mu was confident that he had become a Christian.

Teh Ah Mu was one of the stalwarts who encouraged the church to keep going after the missionaries had to leave. They took turns in leading and preaching, and today he is responsible for evangelism in Ulu Yam.

Grace Lim also experienced strong family opposition when she showed an interest in Christianity. She was six years old when Edith Cork invited her to come to Sunday School. She went along with her brother and sister and was intrigued by these white ladies who spoke her language. She found that she really enjoyed the meetings. However, her father forbade all his children to go back, and he took a chair outside and sat by the gate for the hour of the Sunday School so they could not get past him. But little Grace was very determined and full of ingenuity, and the three of them slipped out the back door and made their way through the muddy lanes without their father ever knowing. Starved of love in the home, it was the loving care the missionaries showed her which drew her week by week.

Nine years and several missionaries later, Grace decided that she wanted to receive Christ as her Saviour. Then the problem faced her: what should she eat, as her mother always placed all the food on the family idol shrine before it went to the table? Because she was eating nothing but biscuits, her mother soon discovered her decision. 'Be a loyal daughter and help your family in every way,' the missionaries had counselled her. And this paid off, even though it involved the disagreeable work of looking after the pigs and cleaning out the pigsty. After a few months her mother relented and put food aside for her.

For many years Grace was the only Christian in the family and had to suffer taunts and ridicule. But when her mother had a heart bypass operation, a Christian nurse shared the gospel with her.

Anxious, but too frightened to believe, her mother asked Grace, 'Will I go to heaven if I die? You are my daughter, I trust you to tell me the truth!'

'Yes, if you put your trust in Jesus,' Grace replied. And so her mother too believed. When she came home a few weeks later, she asked for the idol paraphernalia to be removed, and so her husband sent it all back to the temple.

But Grace's mother died a few weeks later and her father was full of reproaches. 'If your Jesus is so good and true, why did your mother die?' he demanded. Poor Grace had no answer. Her younger siblings and older brother and sister-in-law were also very angry over her mother's death and the removal of all the idols. All Grace could do was keep quiet and cry out to her heavenly Father.

When I saw Grace's happy face and wonderful smile, I marvelled that she had come through so much. Against family pressure she held out for ten years, believing that God would eventually give her a Christian husband. God has blessed them with two grown-up children who follow the Lord. Grace teaches in the Sunbeam Kindergarten run by the church, where they have a free hand to pray with the children and teach Bible stories. She prays often that the parents of her little students will come to know Christ through their children, even as her mother did.

David Ho Lye Heng experienced a hard childhood. 'My whole family suffered a lot when I was a child. We were bullied and almost cast out of the village because we were so poor. At times we didn't have even rice to eat and my poor mother was at the end of her tether.'

David's father had died suddenly, when he was only eight years old and the youngest of the five sons was just five months old. With no social security at that time they were desperate. David and his mother had to find whatever odd jobs and part-time work was available, and this continued right through until his sixth form studies.

After some years, feeling utterly exhausted and almost ready to give up hope, his mother sent David and two brothers to relatives in Rawang and here, for the first time, he heard the gospel. Mr Ong Kian Koen, who had been trained by OMF, was very keen for the Lord and worked hard to spread the gospel. He met David one day and invited him to a Saturday night youth gathering. David recalls that the moment he stepped into the church the warmth and friendliness and welcome made a deep impact on him. He had never before felt such love and concern, and he realized there was something here that he wanted. However, he questioned Fern Blair, Ethel Cork and Mr Ong a great deal before finally making a decision to accept Jesus as his Saviour.

As did so many others, David met huge opposition from his family, who were ardent idol worshippers and wanted their son to carry on the ancestor worship. They were so angry that one day his mother burst out, 'Go and die! If you insist on being a Christian I don't want you as my son.' His friends teased him mercilessly until often he felt like giving up. But Mr Ong lovingly came alongside him and said, 'As Christians this is what we have to face. But you'll find it is worth it in the end.'

Watching how Fern and Ethel lived, David was challenged to see truly humble and holy lives, and this has been an inspiration to him. Over the years he has developed into a fine Christian leader, being made a deacon of Rawang Church and later its chairman. He runs a Christian fellowship in the school where he teaches and helps to guide and train young people. For their church they are daringly planning a new $1.2 million four-storey building with kindergarten and after-school club facilities.

David completed his story by telling us, 'Each time when I recall the sufferings I have faced in my life, I really thank God for everything. Because he wants to train me to be a humble servant of our Lord.'

As we were about to leave this little gathering of Christians in Rawang, I noticed a young mother with her five-year-old child.

'I'm sorry, I haven't asked who you are,' I said.

'My husband is the first missionary sent out from Rawang Church,' she replied simply. 'He's working in Myanmar among the Wa people. He flies to Chiengmai in Thailand and then it's a long dangerous drive because of the fighting. That's why the children and I can't go with him. He goes there for four months and then comes home for two to be with the family.'

I saw a tinge of loneliness on her face. But then she smiled suddenly and added, 'Last month they baptized two hundred people, so it's worth all the partings.'

As I left Rawang I felt deeply humbled by the suffering so many of these early Christians had to face, and by the spirit of sacrifice of this young missionary couple. Truly those who sow in tears shall reap in joy.[96]

11.

The Next Grade Up

Malaysia Bible Seminary

Rawang CTC was beginning to meet the needs of Chinese Christians for training for Christian ministry, but how could those educated in the English language be trained? In 1952 OMF, assisted by local Christians, had sponsored the Singapore Bible College, which was interdenominational and evangelical. This had a strong English section.

But later, because of Singapore's separation from Malaysia in 1965, it became necessary to start a Malaysian college. After much prayer and discussion, evangelical Christians took the bold step of opening a Bible college in Melaka, offering a two-year residential course. Pusat Latihan Kristian Melaka (Malacca Christian Training Centre) was opened in 1976. Reverend Peter Warner, an OMF missionary, was appointed as dean, although the board, consisting mainly of local Christians, still actively looked for a Malaysian principal.

Peter and Ronalda Warner had already served ten years in Grace Presbyterian Church, Batu Pahat. Because Peter was handicapped by a severe hearing problem, his friends had been surprised when he felt called to overseas mission.

'How will he ever learn another language?' they wondered. But God knew there were English-speaking churches full of young people who needed pastoring, and Peter and Ronalda had a fruitful ministry, seeing many coming to Christ and being built up in their faith.

Pusat Latihan Kristian Melaka grew rapidly and two years later developed into the Malaysia Bible Seminary, and the MBS board of directors was officially formed. A Chinese section was also started in Petaling Jaya at that time. Soon the visionary leaders longed for a joint college, with English and Chinese sections together. After much searching and praying, God led them to Luther House in Petaling Jaya, where they continued to meet the needs of many local Christians.

Finding premises in which Christians can meet often presents a big problem in Malaysia. They wanted to purchase their own buildings, and some years later they bought the present premises of several terraced shoplots in Klang. It is far from ideal as a college, as each shoplot has its own staircase and the floors are set at different levels, so it seems a maze of stairs and doorways. But through all the difficulties of constant moves and inadequate buildings, MBS is graduating many fine Christian workers.

From small beginnings the interdenominational MBS now plays an important role in the Malaysian church. It is fully accredited by the Asian Theological Association and offers both undergraduate and postgraduate courses to about three hundred students. They praise the Lord for a strong council of fine local Christians and for their first two Malaysian principals, Reverend Dr Lee Ken Ang and Reverend Dr Tan Kim Sai.

At the same time, the ecumenical Seminari Teologia Malaysia was inaugurated in 1977 to meet the needs of the mainline churches. Cordial relationships between these two colleges led to discussions about a merger, but it was felt best for each to remain separate while co-operating closely together. Today the Malaysian Association of Theological Schools links eight member colleges in warm fellowship.

◆   ◆   ◆   ◆

Dr Tan Kim Sai, MBS principal

Attending one of the many youth retreats in the early 1960s at Rawang CTC was a thirteen-year-old lad called Tan Kim Sai. He used to run about, barefoot and bare-topped, in the streets of the remote New Village of Pendamaran, careless of his behaviour, wanting only to mess about with his friends. Having fun and gambling were the only goals in his life.

But a few years earlier his uncle and family had come to live with them, and the uncle was a Christian. This uncle brought Kim Sai to the small Methodist church that met across the road from their home. Here Olive Finney, an OMF missionary, was serving, and through the Sunday School, scruffy little Kim Sai became a Christian.

Looking back years later, Dr Tan Kim Sai remembers Olive as a wonderfully warm spiritual mother who encouraged him to work hard and develop, both spiritu-ally and academically. With her strong backing, from his unpromising early roots, Tan Kim Sai went on to study and later became a teacher. He fearlessly witnessed with his colleague, Peter Lee, both in school and in the whole neighbouring area. Later these two friends felt the call of God into full-time service and enrolled in OMF's newly sponsored Singapore Bible College.

As a result of this training, Tan Kim Sai's horizons began to expand. He went on to pastor the Chinese Presbyterian church in Batu Pahat. Later he went for further study in Canada, gaining a Master of Missiology degree. This was followed by a Masters degree in Islamic studies in England and a PhD in Inter-cultural studies in America. As principal of the Malaysia Bible Seminary today, one of his goals is to understand Muslims more deeply – a very important aspect of living in a multi-cultural society.

Dr Tan Kim Sai comes over as a strong personality, vibrant and warm, with a ready smile that creases his whole face delightfully. As he described OMF's contribution to the church in Malaysia, Dr Tan Kim Sai stressed the servant-leadership model which was so clearly visible in their missionaries. His fondest memories are of lively and vivacious Olive Finney, who worked unstintingly in the Methodist church without thought of wielding authority or political manoeuvring. Her loving caring spirit permeated all that she did.

Speaking in his strong, confident voice, Dr Tan also stressed OMF's clear-sightedness in seeing the gaps in the local churches and working to fill them. One of the great needs at that time was for systematic biblical teaching. Sadie Custer, a gifted OMF Bible teacher, ably worked to fulfil this task, tirelessly travelling around the small churches and giving clear and challenging teaching on the Bible and Christian stewardship. Tan Kim Sai also remembers being challenged by Olive Finney's in-depth study of the book of Acts and the story of the expansion of the early church as a teenager in Sunday School. David Day's vivid series on Philippians also made a lasting impression on him.

He is grateful, too, for OMF's lead in laying a foundation for the Malaysia Bible Seminary.

Many years later he was challenged by visiting Olive Finney and Sadie Custer. Dr Tan was deeply touched when he learned that they had kept his photo and frequently prayed for him by name. He found such faithfulness in intercession impressive and humbling.

Dr Tan Kim Sai believes that the OMF model of servant leadership, thorough Bible teaching and faithful prayer have laid a solid foundation for the Malaysian church today. We are reminded of the words which Paul wrote to Timothy: 'Do your best to win full approval in God's sight, as a worker who is not ashamed of his work, one who correctly teaches the message of God's truth' (2 Tim. 2:15, Good News Bible).[97]

◆　　　◆　　　◆　　　◆

Formal teaching was not, however, the only way to train young Christians. Many OMF missionaries gave themselves to teaching the Bible, both in mid-week meetings and during the Sunday services. They encouraged as many as they could to work through Bible correspondence courses, and they discipled them in how to do house-to-house visiting, giving out tracts and other forms of evangelism, learning how to preach and developing every aspect of spiritual growth and maturity in Christ.

One outstanding missionary mentor was Peter Young, a Cambridge graduate and an ordained Anglican. He worked with OMF from 1954 to 1957. But then he resigned, feeling that OMF Anglicans were too separatist and OMF was missing the boat by not admitting that the English-speaking work held the key to the evangelization of Malaysia.

When he returned to Malaysia as a free-lance worker, the Anglican bishop found him a place at St Gabriel's

School, Kuala Lumpur, and here Peter started a great work for God. He began a Christian fellowship for the students and later started an English-speaking church on Sundays in the school building. Hundreds of young people came under his Christian influence.

One young man among many who he mentored was Tan Jin Huat.

◆   ◆   ◆   ◆

Reverend Tan Jin Huat

'He was part of us!'

Reverend Tan Jin Huat, pastor of the English-speaking congregation of St Gabriel's Church, Kuala Lumpur, and lecturer at the Malaysian Theological Seminary, could not help smiling at the memory.

'Peter lived just down the road from our home,' Jin Huat continued. 'We were fascinated to see an Englishman cycling to school every day. You know – white men drive cars – and here he was cycling! But he never stood on ceremony, even when he was appointed headmaster. He was very easygoing and relaxed, and we school kids could drop in and visit any time.'

'Were you a Christian then?' I asked.

'Oh yes. I'd been brought up in a Christian home. My father was a Methodist and very devout. Even now I can picture him getting up early and praying fervently out loud in the Chinese style.

'When I was old enough to go to St Gabriel's School I joined the Boys' Brigade. Douglas Sadler was in charge. He was a young OMF missionary who in his youth had been held as a prisoner in China by the Japanese. He encouraged us all to work on our Boys' Brigade badges and study his Bible class material. He'd just got married to Rosy and she taught us first aid. They were a fine couple.

'When I think of Douglas, I think of books. He would always bring books to meetings and urge us to buy them. Wide Christian reading helped us grow spiritually.

'One day Douglas came to visit my home together with a Japanese missionary, Dr Toyotomi, who was conducting an evangelism workshop with the OMF missionaries. They came to visit my older brother. But he was out and they only found me in. Dr Toyotomi asked me if I was a Christian, and he explained Revelation 3:20 very clearly to me – about Jesus standing outside the door of our lives and waiting for us to ask him in. I did just that, and it clinched it for me.'

'So that was your definite step of commitment,' I commented.

'Yes. And studying at St Gabriel's School helped me to grow as a Christian. Peter Young invited lots of interesting speakers. Many of them, like Keith Ranger, were from OMF. He was a key evangelist.

'But the one who made us lads all sit up was Joanne Butts. She was a very trendy American – not the usual sort of OMFer – very modern for those days, wearing lipstick and earrings. Mind you, some thought missionaries shouldn't behave like that!' Jin Huat added with a loud laugh. 'But Peter Young was always radical and encouraged her to be herself. Under his leadership she felt free to introduce new ideas. She started the youth fellowship and then got the Boys' Brigade and the Girls' Brigade to meet with them and hold combined meetings. Sometimes 150 or 200 young people came. I was president, and we all felt it was wonderful to have so many worshipping and learning together. Some came from really tough non-Christian homes and they needed encouragement. And some were not yet Christians at all.

'Peter recognized that guitars and a music group are a good way to attract youngsters. So some of us started the Singing Saints under the leadership of Lee Wai Kong. It became very popular. I joined when I was about sixteen and we had a great time. We visited lots of church youth fellowships, singing and sharing our faith. I remember going to Sepang, Sungai Way, and even as far north as Penang and down south to Kluang when Henry and Mary Guinness were working there. As we ministered we also acted as counsellors to the young people. Of course at that stage we didn't know much ourselves, but it certainly challenged us to grow spiritually.

'Peter was our pastor. In those days St Gabriel's was really just a youth church. But he stretched us and gave us responsibility, together with the space to carry it out. Hungry for a strong foundation for our Christian life, we all began to read widely. One day when I was in the Evangel Book Centre I bought a copy of In Understanding Be Men.[98] This gave me a good start in the study of Christian doctrine. And later those of us on the lay readers course signed up for the Australian College of Theology. Peter gave us the books to read and then paid for us to sit the exam.

'I'm afraid we never thought about the fee – he must have quietly paid it for us,' Jin Huat added with a deprecatory smile. 'Or perhaps the church paid, I'm not quite sure. And by the time I was at university, aged nineteen, Peter was beginning to have us preach. This was to be the beginning of my life as a preacher.

'You see, Peter was very perceptive. It was the late 1960s and the ten-year-rule had just been announced: foreigners could stay a maximum of ten years in Malaysia. They must work themselves out of a job, training a local person. Peter challenged us: "the missionaries are leaving but the fields are white to harvest. We need local people to pick up the challenge!" So a number of us seriously began to consider going into full-time Christian work. In fact, from St Gabriel's at that time I should think 15 or 20 young people went into full-time ministry for Christ.

'The first one was my friend Mau Onn, who led the Singing Saints. He was very gifted. Got a first-class honours. Peter encouraged him to go to Australia to study under Leon Morris. But sadly he settled down in a Chinese church in Perth and didn't come back to Malaysia for years.

'That totally changed Peter's ideas about theological study and studying overseas. In fact, at that time crowds of people were migrating – every month we heard of some other key Christian who left – especially after the race riots in May 1969. Peter was very direct. He used to say, "How is it that people are always called to the better countries, not places like India or Cambodia?"

'We were further challenged to consider full-time ministry by the example of Spring Ho from Hong Kong. She was a student in training at the Singapore Discipleship Training Centre and worshipped for a while at St Gabriel's. She was also a graduate, which was an encouragement for those of us with a university education. She became one of the early Asian missionaries.'

'So what happened to you?' I asked.

'I worked for three years after university and then joined the staff of the Fellowship of Evangelical Students (FES). This movement was strategic in reaching university students, many of whom became the future leaders of the Malaysian church. Then John Chew, who is now the Anglican Bishop of Singapore and the Archbishop of the Province of South East Asia, encouraged me to join him in studying at Trinity College, Bristol. And so eventually I joined the staff of the Malaysia Bible Seminary

(MBS) and was dean of the English department for 15 years. Now, of course, I lecture at the Theological Seminary (STM), the seminary sponsored by the main-line denominations – Anglican, Methodist, Lutheran and Presbyterian. Over the years many of us have studied for theological doctorates, so that our seminary and Bible college is almost entirely staffed by Malaysians.'

'So, looking back, what influence do you feel OMF had on you and your contemporaries?' I asked.

'When I think of OMF, I think of a serving ministry. They were incarnational – it was their lives which challenged us, as they became one of us. This is what I remember: the open home, the warm welcome at any time of day, the listening ear when we needed it. They had a big impact on young people, even in the villages. And of course many young people migrated to the towns and became leaders in the churches there.

'But OMF probably didn't realize early enough how strategic the towns were,' he added thoughtfully. 'They took some persuading to move to the towns. Some of us felt they were rather too slow about this. However, afterwards they had some key people working in towns. And for our student meetings OMF would supply really helpful speakers like the charismatic David Adeney, who had been a student worker in China. Their missionaries also spoke at Camp Cameron – the one-month leadership training course which the Malaysian Fellowship of Evangelical Students organized each vacation.'

Jin Huat paused for a moment's thought. 'I guess their key ministry was training emerging leaders. But I would say that their main weakness was that with their focus on evangelism they tended to ignore the role of Christians in secular work. It was as if full-time Christian work was the highest ideal and anything else was second best. So at university we struggled to square our Christian faith with a work ethic. But FES stepped into that gap. Sharing and learning together in their meetings at university gave us a wider view of life.'

After talking with the Reverend Tan Jin Huat I thanked God for older Christians who saw the potential in a group of school kids and encouraged and taught them. I was excited that so many of these youngsters have grown into mature Christian leaders today. Their vision, spirituality and zeal for mission present a challenge to the church worldwide. Every church needs the eyes of faith to see the potential in someone else.[99]

12.

Widening the Vision

'A big Hindu festival is going to take place in a few days, don't you think we should try and take some Christian literature there too?'

Mary Welander,[100] another OMF missionary who had been forcibly deported from China, always felt her first love was the Chinese. They were the priority for her mission, and the existing churches consisted largely of Chinese. But the dark-skinned Indians she met on her travels throughout Malaya began to tug at her heart. Many were Tamils from south India, brought over by the British to do hard labour in the tin mines and the poorly paid work of rubber tapping. A few more educated Indians were also to be found in white-collar jobs in the cities.

Not knowing what to expect, Mary and a few Chinese and western friends loaded her small car with Tamil and English gospels and tracts and set out for the Batu Caves. Huge caves set high in some limestone cliffs eight miles from Kuala Lumpur form a magnet for some sixty thousand Hindus who travel from all over the country to celebrate their annual festival of Thaipusam.

As they neared the site, there was so much traffic that they were crawling, three vehicles abreast, along the little road leading to the caves. A stream of buses was also arriving, full of people in their best clothes, the bright colours of the saris glowing cheerfully against the women's black hair. A train, travelling constantly back and forth from the capital, kept disgorging capacity crowds.

At last Mary managed to find a parking space and they all got out. Radios were blaring and entertainment of every kind surrounded them. Everything imaginable was on sale – balloons, ice cream, drinks for the thirsty – there was even a car being raffled for $1 tickets. All manner of paraphernalia for idol worship crowded the stalls.

But other things caught her eye, too. The ground near her was stained red, like dried congealed blood. Startled, she realized it came from the betel-nut which the women chewed and then spat out wherever they walked. Men and women, boys and girls were completing their ritual ablutions in the river and beginning to make their way up the 350 steps towards the shrine. Some were crawling, painfully, on their knees, hoping that their suffering would atone for their sins.

She saw semi-naked holy men daubed with red and yellow dyes slowly dancing along the road. The dulling hypnosis of the regular beat of drums and the shouts of their escorts kept these spirit-possessed people moving relentlessly towards the temple enclosure. There were little girls among them too, also in a trance, and she saw they had skewers pushed through their cheeks. Horrified, the group of Christians watched as even more extreme devotees followed along in the procession. They had enormous coloured frames (kavadi) held high above their heads, supported by forty spikes pushed into the skin all over their bodies. Yet there was no sign of blood. Others walking barefoot, but apparently unhurt, across long pits of red-hot coals, revealed what the powers of evil can do.

The long procession moved down the broad drive and then slowly climbed the long flight of steps.

The little group of Christians felt the atmosphere of evil and shuddered at the cruelty and the agonized looks on some of the faces. The sight of little children in the midst of such demonic activity made Mary feel sick.

They turned away from the procession and went over to the spectators, offering their Gospels for sale or urging people to take a free tract. All day long they worked until they were exhausted, sunburnt and footsore. And as they worked, they prayed that the seeds of the gospel being sown would bring fruit some day. But wherever they went there appeared to be no Tamil-speaking Christian witnessing to the crowds, and Mary prayed that the small Tamil churches would grow and see the desperate needs of their own people.

Mary wrote, 'From then on, every red earth road that led off the main road out into a rubber estate was a challenge to compassion for these "other sheep" whom the Lord loved.' Living in dingy rows of small wooden or concrete houses, tens of thousands of Tamils struggled to make ends meet on their meagre pay. Children ran wild with no one to care for them while the adults left before dawn to tap the trees. At night the scanty wage was often squandered on drinking toddy made from coconuts. What could Chinese-speaking missionaries do for these needy people?

There were already a number of Tamil churches in some towns, largely the fruit of Methodist evangelism, but there were not nearly enough to reach the hundreds of thousands of immigrant workers. Multitudes of Indians had still never heard of Christ. Recognizing this great unmet need, OMF made arrangements for two mature Tamil-speaking missionary couples to come from India and help to set up a Tamil programme. Loaned by the Strict Baptists, the Orchards and the Kuhrts moved to Johor State and began reaching out to the many railway workers and those on the rubber estates. Their fluency in the language was particularly valued. This also represented a model of inter-mission co-operation. Several new OMFers were designated to study the Tamil language and work alongside these more experienced missionaries, while Tamil Christians were challenged to share the vision with their own people.

Wherever she could, Mary would visit Tamil as well as Chinese- and English-speaking schools and was happy to see her ten-cent Gospels selling well.

> At one such school I learnt a lesson in relinquishing. A little Tamil schoolboy offered to carry a box of books to my car. He seemed so thin and small that I hesitated. He had a runny nose and a bad cough, but he was so eager to help and so afraid of being rejected. So I let him.
>
> He staggered to the car and dumped the heavy box inside. With a breathless smile he burst out proudly. 'Teacher, I carried it myself!' Bless him! He had taught me a valuable lesson. I must not look at the small Tamil church or the weakness of its witnesses. I must let them carry responsibility and serve God themselves.

God worked in some unusual ways among the Tamils. Mat was only nine when he trusted Christ as his Saviour. He attended a Christian school and often visited his classmates, sitting on their doorsteps and chatting about Christ. No one knows how many playmates became Christians through him.

Then suddenly he was taken ill and died three days later. His family buried him with Hindu rites, but the school arranged a Christian memorial service. Twenty-one of his Hindu relatives attended and heard the gospel for the first time. His only Christian relative was an aunt who bought Tamil New Testaments to give to everyone after the service. Within a year three of the family members had become Christians and several more were attending meetings. In her account Mary commented on the marvel of how even after death little Mat was still making an impact.

As the OMF team of Tamil workers grew, so the opportunities increased. A flood near Banting meant that hundreds crowded into the big Methodist school for safety. Bill and Joanne Harris, OMF missionaries, thoughtfully brought a large cauldron of boiling water for them, and this provided a new opening. As a result, two Bible classes were held each week on the Brooklands estate with 15 men at one and 70 children at the other. Bill was then given openings in the Tamil High School and found he had the opportunity to teach the Bible to seven hundred students each week. Besides all this, eight young people came at 7 a.m. four times a week to study Matthew's Gospel.

Because they were so poor, many Tamils were willing to sacrifice the interests of a whole family in order to give one member – usually a son – the best education possible. Ben Orchard described how he encountered this one day.[101]

An old man was browsing through their books and asked for John's Gospel. Knowing he could not read, Ben asked him what he would do with the book.

'*We* are going to read,' he replied, using a pronoun which excluded the listener.

'Who are *we*?' Ben asked. 'May *we* (using an inclusive pronoun) read also?' The man gladly fixed a time for Ben to visit, and when he saw Ben coming he called out to his son to come in. The son was an attractive lad, about eighteen years old, and he soon engaged Ben in animated conversation in English. His education contrasted sharply with that of his illiterate parents and semi-literate siblings.

The father spread rush mats on the floor and called his whole family to gather round. Then his son started to read from John's Gospel, pausing only to re-read any passage his father had not grasped. The clearly pronounced and properly emphasized words were a joy for Ben to hear.

But that was not all. The old man now took up the story and began to question his family. No one escaped his searching voice. Sons, daughters and wife were all catechized on the reading. Ben sat back, marvelling at the old man's grasp of the material and his ability to probe the minds of others.

But it would not be easy for a Tamil to become a Christian. After many months of work, Ben Orchard listed some of the difficulties he was encountering.[102] The Tamils were a tight-knit community, holding their family traditions and four thousand-year-old religion in great respect. Anyone wishing to leave Hinduism would face severe ostracism and probably violence, and many falsehoods and slanders would be spread against them. Tamils would listen eagerly to any discussion about the nature of God. But moving on to the personal issues of sin and the need for salvation would immediately arouse hostility. Ben knew full well that Hindus were not averse to syncretism – Jesus could happily be added to their plethora of gods. But Ben often found that someone who showed an interest would not be there next time he visited.

'He's gone back to India,' he would be informed, or 'He moved to another estate' – which was a common occurrence. The mobility of the Tamil population made following up various contacts rather discouraging. He could only pray that where he had planted the seed, someone else would water – and that God would give the harvest one day.

After some years, the Orchards left Malaysia for family reasons and the Kuhrts wanted to spend their last years before retirement back in India. So it was decided that the best way forward would be for the OMF Tamil work to link up with Tamil-speaking Methodist churches in the towns. But as the Methodists were generally more highly educated and professional people from higher castes, they often found it difficult to relate to rubber-tappers and tin miners. So the Methodist churches discipled the Christians but left OMF the responsibility for evangelism. The preparation of Christian education material was another ministry which OMF undertook, together with nationwide women's work. By co-operating in this way, the Tamil churches were invigorated and enriched, and the OMF missionaries learnt much from their Indian colleagues.

There were other Indian races in Malaysia as well, chief among them the Malayali, who came from the strongly Christian areas around Kerala. These Mar Thoma Christians proudly traced their faith right back to the Apostle Thomas who, according to tradition, evangelized parts of south India. When Martin and I lived in Kluang in the 1960s we made friends with a young Mar Thoma minister. He confided to Martin that, despite years of theological training, he felt inadequately trained for his calling because his theological training back in India had included very little biblical content.

'Come visit us,' Martin suggested, 'and we can do some Bible study together. Bring your Greek New Testament and we'll work through an epistle. That will do me good, too, as my Greek is on the back burner now that I am thinking in Malay.'

The two men were about the same age and really enjoyed the stimulus of weekly study together.

'I'm just starting a monthly service in English,' the Mar Thoma minister told Martin. 'If you could come and preach for me that would be great.'

Martin leapt at the opportunity and so the friendship grew.

These services in English were fairly simple, but a full Mar Thoma service was quite a different matter. When Martin was invited by another Mar Thoma pastor to preach in his church, which was much larger, he enquired what time the service started.

'Come about twelve o'clock and preach for an hour,' was his casual reply.

'All right, but when does the service start?'

'Oh, come at twelve, that's fine,' he replied. It took Martin a while to winkle out of him that most people would gather around nine o'clock, but the liturgy was long and involved and would all be in Malayali. There was no need for Martin to be there at the beginning.

Intrigued, we arrived about eleven o'clock, and what a colourful sight met our eyes. Several hundred worshippers were packed into the church, and crowds spilled outside onto the wide veranda that surrounded the church on three sides. The women, sitting in groups in the shade and keeping an eye on the children or nursing their babies, wore beautiful saris of all colours. There was a relaxed and friendly atmosphere as they half-listened to the service inside.

We were welcomed immediately and taken to some seats at the front of the church. Our friend the priest was arrayed in gorgeous robes which he changed from time to time as he moved between the high altar and the congregation. The swinging incense and the chanting of the choir filled the building with an ethereal atmosphere, while the acolytes, dressed also in rich apparel, moved purposefully about their business.

I gazed at the scene before me and suddenly began to smile in spite of myself. Right in front of us stood a large acolyte, dressed in his ornate robes. He had taken his shoes off and we could see his vividly coloured socks. Rings of orange, green and red embraced his foot and ankle – and a big brown toe projected through a hole in his sock.

'This is all so different,' I whispered to Martin. 'All this ritual and tradition. Do you think they want our type of evangelical preaching?'

Martin whispered back, 'I've been having to learn that in the west we associate ritual with liberal teaching. But they don't necessarily have to go together. I think these people will be hungry for spiritual teaching.'

And so they were. They hung on every word Martin said, and after the service the bag of Christian books we had brought was sold in a flash. The next morning the elder came to us with a long list of more books that various members had ordered. We were learning that OMF had a ministry far beyond just the Chinese New Villages.

The Indian races in Malaysia not only form their own strong churches, but many of them are scattered throughout the largely Chinese churches. I had the privilege to meet and interview one of them, the Reverend Robin Arumugam.

♦   ♦   ♦   ♦

Reverend Robin Arumugam

Robin Arumugam entered the office of St John's Anglican Church, Ipoh, radiating geniality and confidence. 'Sorry to have kept you waiting, but life is full,' he explained to Mong and me. 'Let's go out and get something to eat.'

Robin Arumugam is a mature Indian Christian, gifted in leadership and organization. He worked as a consultant trainer in insurance and corporate companies for many years and has also been ordained as a non-stipendiary minister. When Dr Lim Cheng Ean was enthroned as Bishop of West Malaysia, Robin was made master of ceremonies of the thanksgiving dinner programme.

We settled down to some tasty local snacks in one of Robin's favourite Indian cafés. As Robin talked about the early days after he first became a Christian, his emphasis was on the fun they all had together.

'A lot of new missionaries came to the town of Teluk Anson to do language study when Bob Harper was in charge. We used to go with them on cycle rides and picnics to Bidor waterfall and other beauty spots. And then we would help them with tracting and showing films in the various nearby villages. Sometimes I would even cycle over to Tapah, which is 30 miles away, and help George Williamson and Don Temple there. In fact we used to do crazy things, like cycle up to the Cameron Highlands and then freewheel all the way down!'

Robin's zest for life came across in all he said. He had been brought up as a Hindu, and a friend had been urging him to come to the Christian youth fellowship for nine months before he was willing to try. Happily, as his father was working with westerners, he did not object to his son attending meetings. Once committed to the Lord, Robin has never looked back.

'OMF had a great impact on the young people,' Robin reminisced. 'They really cared for us. They helped some people facing exams, for example, with tuition. And all of us were taught how to do evangelism and tracting and door-to-door work. They were not shy. They would talk to everyone. And I'm just the same – I talk to everyone. I don't argue with them, I just share what my Christian faith means to me.'

Robin is happily married to Ruth and they have two daughters who are actively involved in music ministry. One of them was in England, doing a year of mission work in Wellington. Robin was ordained eleven years ago, and he now serves as vicar in charge of St Mary's Chapel, Tambun Road, Ipoh. Most of the congregation come from Sarawak and work in the army camp. He runs a full programme of Sunday School, youth fellowship, women's fellowship, Bible studies and the regular services on Sundays and Fridays, ably assisted by others. Robin also helps out at St John's Church, Ipoh, whose congregation is 80 per cent Indian. He is a synod representative and serves on the diocesan court as well as doing a lot of training in the diocese.

Robin recalled the Scripture Union Camps to which the OMF missionaries would take their young people. 'At my first camp there happened to be Lim Cheng Ean, who is the present Bishop of West Malaysia; Ponniah Moses, now our assistant bishop; Batumalai, the present Archdeacon of Melaka; Jimmy Chee, who is PA to the bishop; Reverend Michael Chee, who is now in Australia; Yeoh Beng San, who is now a doctor and a non-stipendiary minister here in Ipoh, and myself.'

What a list of influential people, I thought to myself. Did those early workers ever dream they were making such an impact?

As we reflected on our fascinating talk with Robin Arumugam, Mong and I agreed how important it is to invest time in the teenagers and young people. One never knows what key ministries they will have in the future.

The Apostle Paul clearly realized this when he called first John Mark and then Timothy to join him in his ministry. Paul acknowledged years later what a help Mark was to him (2 Tim. 4:11), and he encouraged Timothy by saying, 'Don't let anyone look down on you because you are young, but set an example for the believers, in speech, in life, in love, in faith and in purity . . . Be diligent in these matters; give yourself wholly to them, so that everyone may see your progress' (1 Tim. 4:12, 15).

And here, in Ipoh, Mong and I had met someone who perfectly exemplified the outcome of such an investment in younger workers.[103]

13.

Outreach to Those Educated in English

'Have you heard what Cecil and Lucinda Gracey are doing now?' an OMF missionary exclaimed indignantly. 'They're giving up on the hard slog of village evangelism and are moving to the comforts of Johor Bahru.'

'No! Really? What could have possessed them to do that?'

'And what's more,' the speaker continued, 'they're moving into English-speaking ministry! After spending all those years trying to master Hakka, they're not using it any more. I call that a waste.'

'How will the evangelistic teams manage without Cecil's brilliant sketch board? And he has such a sense of humour, the Chinese love him. You can't really mean that they are abandoning the New Villages for town work. That's not what OMF was called to when we first came here!'

When the OMF leaders began to realize the potential of English-speaking ministry, many missionaries, feeling the mission was betraying its original vision, raised their voices in opposition. Other missions might do the 'easy' town work, but we were called to pioneer where it was really difficult. Mere church work couldn't be as important as church planting and 'reaching the unreached'.

Missionaries who give up everything and go to the far reaches of the earth are very often people of strong convictions. Their situation forces them to think for themselves and hold clear, definite views. So criticism of the leaders' policies and of one another's approaches can too easily creep in. But after more than a decade of working in Malaysia, it was high time that OMF recognized the strategic opportunity which work in the English language provided.

Increasingly, English was becoming the language of worldwide education and commerce. Malaysian parents were beginning to realize that if they wanted their children to progress in the future they needed to have an English education. The government, too, was very aware of this and was developing many English-speaking schools. Families with the most initiative and leadership potential began sending their children to these new schools.

OMF had a few couples facing the weary wait for visas to Indonesia, and several of them found a welcome in the Presbyterian churches of Johor, where English-speaking congregations were being formed. In 1965 Martin and I found the political situation made it impossible for us to return to Indonesia, so we joined the 'Indonesia-waiters', filling in time working with the small English-speaking congregation in Kluang.

Dorothy Marx had also, some ten years before, been waiting for her Indonesian visa and therefore had not studied Chinese. She was the one who started this church. Dorothy was a German Jew who had lost most of her family in the Holocaust. Though slight in frame, she abounded in energy and brilliance. She slept just a few hours each night, and it was rumoured that she ate almost nothing except a few peanuts. Later, while attached to an Indonesian-speaking Chinese church, she used her skills as a gifted pianist and organized an evangelistic choir touring Indonesia. For many years she has now served as the principal of an evangelical seminary in Bandung.

I well remember visiting her one time when she was desperately ill and not thinking clearly. Her conversation slipped between the four languages in which she felt at home – German, English, Hebrew and Indonesian. It was difficult to follow her if one did not know at least three out of the four languages.

Dorothy had gathered a few children together who knew English and taught them some Bible stories. Other missionaries came and went and the group began to grow. The missionaries before Martin and I came were a much-loved Brethren couple who practised believer's baptism and taught a clear doctrine of 'once saved, always saved'.

This group of English-speaking high school students met in the Chinese Presbyterian Church and consisted largely of the Presbyterian Christians' own children. So there was a clash of perspectives between Brethren and Presbyterian practices. Much discussion took place as to what was the best way forward, especially as all the other English-speaking churches in Johor State were Presbyterian. Eventually Martin and I found ourselves in the anomalous situation of being asked to oversee a Brethren fellowship changing into a Presbyterian church – and we were Anglicans!

Unknown to us at the time, these English-speaking churches held one of the keys to the growth of Christianity in Malaysia. From them sprang many of the gifted leaders of the future. Dynamic and well taught biblically, these congregations later grew from strength to strength.

But Martin and I felt rather dismayed at first. We had come from a fast-growing group of churches in North Sumatra that had added five thousand new converts in two years.[104] Now we were faced with a congregation of barely 50 people, and most of them were high school students. The oldest member was only twenty-eight years old. Our big challenge was how to attract older people into a church of teenagers, especially when there were few adults around who spoke English. Martin spent time cultivating a friendship with one Mar Thoma Christian man, the only middle-aged person we knew who spoke English.

The Saturday afternoon Bible School was the main event of the week. So shortly after arriving we added a Sunday evening service. We pitched it a little over the heads of our young people and hoped they would grad-uate into it. They were in danger of feeling too old for Christianity once they left school.

From the earlier missionaries we had inherited a large wooden house with a huge attic as our home. The rent was very low as the house was said to be haunted because there was a misshapen tree standing next to our grounds. It had probably been struck by lightning, but the local folk associated it with evil spirits. Also up our lane lived a strange older woman whom our children nicknamed Auntie Longnails. She had made a vow not to cut the nails of her left hand. They were by that time at least three inches long, painted bright red, and looked like the horrible talons of a bird of prey. But as a family we prayed over our surroundings and I felt no qualms about living there.

As did many of our missionary friends, we decorated the walls of our living room with Christian posters and pictures of Bible stories, praying that these would act as conversation openers. Martin and I also kept a table of

Christian books for our church members to buy. Visitors were constantly dropping in so there was little privacy, but we encouraged them all to come.

Martin hit on the idea of holding mini-conferences in our home. We invited our young friends to come after lunch on Friday (the main holiday) and leave before lunch on Saturday. In this way we would only have to give them breakfast and one main meal and need only charge each one 30 cents, which even a school kid could afford. The few church members who were earning contributed a little more.

Our aim was to give them fun, fellowship and teaching, so we packed the programme full. There was space for good teaching slots as well as a great variety of games, while the evening and early morning quiet times gave an opportunity for older Christians to encourage younger ones. If we had more girls than boys, the girls would sleep on the mattresses in the large attic and the boys would crowd into our two spare bedrooms. They never seemed to mind how crowded they were – in fact, it all added to the fun.

In addition to these monthly mini-conferences, Pan-Johor conferences were held every school holiday. Students gathered from Johor Bahru, Batu Pahat, Muar and Kluang, taking it in turns to host the gathering. When that responsibility fell to Kluang we hired the Chinese school at the end of our road and the pupils slept on the desks. It proved tremendously encouraging to meet young Christians from other towns, to hear of their hopes and struggles, and to grow together in deeper discipleship. In 1965 the Muar young people chose worldwide mission as their theme – it was the first time the challenge of overseas mission had been brought to these youthful churches, indeed probably to any church in Malaysia. This became an annual feature in Muar for a number of years.

The welcome and acceptance the young people found also attracted them to the church. Many of them experienced very little love and appreciation in their own homes. Martin and I realized this one day when our little son Andrew, aged three, ran in excitedly and announced, 'I've seen a butterfly!' As wonderful tropical butterflies were common all round us, this was hardly a new discovery. But, much to the amazement of our young guests, Martin replied, 'Have you, darling? What colour was it?' and proceeded to enthuse about his discovery. One of our visitors commented afterwards, 'If I had announced to my father that I had seen a butterfly, he would have been scathing and made me feel so small. But you really encourage your children, don't you?'

But all was not plain sailing. Tragically, one of our young church members, returning home late at night long after his family had gone to bed, attempted to climb in over the garage roof. Something gave way and he crashed through the hole between the rafters and hit his head on the cement floor. When his parents ran in to see what had caused all the noise they found him lying dead on the floor.

News of this tragedy spread quickly through the small town, and many members of our youth fellowship were deeply shocked. To the traditional Chinese mind, death could be a frightening experience. The custom was to lay the body out with a lighted candle at each corner of the bed. They put up Taoist pictures of the afterlife around the room. These vividly portrayed the torments of hell with gory scenes of demonic torture. In this way most children would grow up with a terrible fear of dying.

We were so grateful that Martin was allowed to give this young man a Christian funeral. The glorious message of eternal life with our Lord Jesus Christ shone in bright contrast to the Taoist hopelessness and fear.

One member of our Kluang fellowship found God leading him in unexpected ways.

◆   ◆   ◆   ◆

Poh Pai Peck: Missionary from East to West

'I see every difficulty as an opportunity for evangelism.'

I had not met the speaker for many years, and it was a tremendous joy to see his beaming bespectacled face. Poh Pai Peck, later known as Timothy Poh, was eighteen years old when Martin and I first met him in Kluang in 1965. As a vibrant young leader on our church committee he attracted our attention very early on. Pai Peck's family, including ten siblings, lived on a housing estate in the poorer end of the town. Until the river was dredged and deepened, their home flooded to a metre deep every rainy season. His father was a lorry driver and there was no money for extras such as developing Pai Peck's wonderful musical talents. He had never had a piano lesson, yet we would hear him play the opening movement of a Beethoven sonata nearly perfectly after having listened to a recording.

When we met him in London in 2005 we asked about his music. He told us that he had recently bought a violin and found that he could easily play it.

'You see, I play the guitar, and that helps a lot,' was his modest disclaimer.

'But what brought you to London?' I asked. 'And how did you come to pastor and rebuild Queen's Park United Reformed Church on this busy street just a mile from Wormwood Scrubs?'

'I worked hard and saved enough for a one-way ticket to England just at the time you were leaving Kluang,' Pai Peck, now known as Timothy, replied simply. 'When I arrived I only had £7.10s in my pocket, and just one jumper and one extra shirt and a pair of trousers in my case.'

Life in London proved very hard for Timothy as he tried to put himself through 'A' levels and university. He struggled to find jobs and worked as a petrol pump attendant, a night watchman, and a cleaner, with no holidays. He sometimes held down two or three jobs at once. He met a friendly Chinese supermarket manager and worked every evening after classes, seven days a week. In return he was given his food and £10 a week and allowed to kip down in the tiny attic reached by a rickety ladder. His annual fees for North London Polytechnic at that time were £250. He lived very frugally and carefully saved his £10 each week.

Timothy's heart was for evangelism, yet when he searched the notice boards of the polytechnic he found no mention of a Christian Union meeting. He and two friends went to see the bursar.

'May we have a list of the names and addresses of all the students here?' they asked. They worked their way through the two thousand names on the list, contacting each one and talking to them about Christ. By the time he graduated, a flourishing Christian Union of between fifty and a hundred students was established.

'But you were a maths graduate,' I said. 'How did you come to be an URC pastor?'

This story was equally amazing. He was walking along Fulham High Street one day, when something drew him into Fulham URC church. It was drab, Victorian, and had a dark vestibule. Timothy saw only six elderly people with no pastor to lead them. Taken aback by the totally unpromising situation, he asked the Lord, 'Why did you want me to visit this church?'

'It's here I want you to stay,' came the surprising reply.

The cultural gap between these traditional elderly Londoners and the fresh-faced young Chinese Christian was huge. 'How will they accept me?' Timothy wondered. 'And how will I ever understand them?'

'My first blunder,' he reminisced, 'came about when they were planning a jumble sale. "I'll make some cakes for you," I offered, not understanding at all that home-made cakes were not usually part of a jumble sale!'

But their laughter broke the ice and he began to win their hearts. Timothy's enthusiasm proved infectious and soon they asked him to take a lead and numbers began to grow.

'Come and be our pastor,' they urged him.

Timothy recollected a crisis he had faced years before in Malaysia when he had told God he was willing to do anything for him – even, horror of horrors, becoming a missionary to Africa. Now he felt God telling him clearly this was God's plan: he should train for ordination. But he had only just completed five years of intensive study while working night and day to earn his keep. Now that he had graduated, his family back home were expecting regular financial support from him. And one of his many brothers had recently arrived and needed help with trav-elling the same path of study and finding jobs. Wasn't it time to ease up a little?

But for Timothy, God's work came before everything else. He enrolled in a course training URC ministers. It would involve three years of evening classes, intensive input at the weekends and some holiday study weeks. Every Sunday he would lead the services, preach and play the piano for the hymns. Timothy certainly never shied away from hard work.

Under Timothy's leadership, and with a growing con-gregation, Fulham URC tore down the old Victorian building and replaced it with an attractive modern church building.

Queen's Park URC met in another dilapidated Victorian building, and for over 20 years had had no minister. They pleaded with Pastor Timothy to come and do the same for them: revive and build up the congregation.

'How did you find the energy to start all over again?' I asked him.

'I always like a challenge,' he said with a smile, 'but it nearly finished me off. They wanted to rebuild, but we learnt that English Heritage held the church to be a listed building, and it took three years of complicated negotiating to un-list it. You can't imagine the hassle! We even had to find homes for the huge iron supporting pillars, and we managed to sell the organ to an American church.'

Once that hurdle was cleared, with Timothy's financial skills they raised the money for the demolition and rebuilding by selling off part of the land for flats. And they also built a manse right next door, which is rented out and brings in a steady income, as Timothy is still living frugally elsewhere.

Utterly exhausted by all his responsibilities, Timothy decided to take a year out, during which he would worship at his old church in Fulham. But he soon noticed the crying needs of the young people there who had no one to lead them. With his gifting and energy, Timothy was soon running all the youth work, from Sunday School to older teenagers, arranging camps and other weekend activities. As the year progressed he also became involved in the Camden Chinese Community Centre and rescued them from near-bankruptcy. He has been their chairman now for seven years.

Back at Queen's Park URC, Pastor Timothy now leads a warm and friendly congregation of about 50 adults.

And what an international mix they are. We met Afro-Caribbeans, Indians, French, Germans, Chinese and many others.

'This congregation has faith that God can work,' Timothy commented, 'and that's what I like about them. But because we are not one of the larger Congregational churches they won't spare us a minister when I retire. People are basically selfish, you know,' he continued. 'All the pastors want the better churches. They are all cherry-picking!'

'But,' he went on brightly, 'I'm fifty-nine now, so I have about six more years, and I've worked out a plan. I'm going to run a Bible training course for my congregation. We'll teach what Christian discipleship really means. I'll develop their confidence to lead Bible studies and eventually preach. There will be group leadership, so they can support each other. I've also written to several Bible colleges to ask if one of their students can help. There's room in the church to turn into a small flat, and the income from the manse could provide a small salary.'

As I looked into Pastor Timothy's face it showed telltale lines of strain due to the tremendous pressure under which he had worked all these years. What a challenge his dedication to the Lord he loves is to the many half-hearted Christians in the West.

I asked if he ever felt lonely. He had told me he never had time to think about marriage. Behind his gentle unassuming ways I had seen a born leader, brimming with gifts, who had given his whole life to the unglamorous task of resurrecting two run-down churches in faraway London. He is a true missionary from East to West. As the Malaysian church reaches out to the wider world through him, the early work of OMF in Malaysia is bearing good fruit back in Britain.[105]

14.

Developing Dynamic Leadership and Growth

The young Christians in Kluang looked up to the Batu Pahat folk as having the more mature Christians. When Malcolm and Anne Ryland-Jones were appointed to Batu Pahat in 1963 those young people soon indicated that they were very good at running their own services and did not see any need for missionary oversight. Well over 50 youngsters gathered for their meetings, and the enthusiastic and efficient leaders were very good at inviting their friends.

Malcolm and Anne settled in quietly to bide their time. The home chosen for them was far from ideal. The family on one side knocked bugs out of their bed boards each morning, while those on the other side kept them awake until the early hours with the noise and smell of their late night meals as they celebrated their religious festivals. During their first wet season they realized why their house had been the last one in the terrace to sell. The communal cesspool was located in their backyard and overflowed with an abundance of cockroaches as it filled with water![106]

But the Ryland-Joneses persevered and soon discovered that the young people had a tremendous hunger for God's truth. They were able to have a rich and fulfilling ministry of teaching and training among them. The two leading lights among the young people were Micky Kua (who we met earlier) and Richard Tok, both university students at that time. They were exceptionally gifted in organization and administration, and when they spoke they were skilled in opening up the Scriptures.

After Malcolm's ordination in 1966, the English Presbyterian Church formed a Deacon's Court and was able to raise sufficient funds to call a graduate from Singapore Bible College the following year. God's plans and purposes for that youth group were wonderfully realized in the new Grace Presbyterian Church.

In the following years, under the dynamic leadership of Reverend Wong Fong Yang, Grace Presbyterian Church grew by leaps and bounds. It has become a key church in the wider area.

Grace Presbyterian Church

Today Grace Presbyterian Church, Batu Pahat, has its own magnificent building, in a prominent position on the top of a hill where a huge red cross on the spire can be seen from far away. To gain permission to build was no easy matter. It took them ten years of persistent prayer and negotiating with the government before the site was granted. And even then the height had to be reduced, lest it proved to be taller than the local mosque. When Peter Warner, who took up the work of the Ryland-Joneses a few years later, returned to Malaysia and first saw the building, he said he felt like the Queen of Sheba when she saw the glory of Solomon's palaces, 'her breath was knocked out of her'.

The auditorium is large enough to seat four hundred worshippers and is complete with audio and visual equipment. The building also has offices for the pastor, the assistant pastor and the administrator, together with Sunday School rooms and space for a Malay language service run by a pastor from Sarawak. They send teams from time to time over to Sarawak in support of the tribal churches. They have also started services in Vietnamese to reach out to the local migrant workers. And, in a strange twist as they are an essentially English-speaking congregation, they have added a Chinese language service as well.

A kindergarten with six classes takes place on the premises too, reaching out to the local children. What's more, they have now pulled down the house where the Warner family used to live and built an 'Early Intervention Centre' for up to 25 children with special needs. It is sponsored, staffed and supported by Grace Church alone. An Elderly Persons' Home has recently been added, and a student centre and hostel set up just five miles away in Parit Raja.

The church leaders believe that God has many more opportunities for ministry for them, and they look to him in faith for guidance and provision as the work expands.

Many of the original young people are now leaders in various churches. Richard Tok became the general secretary of the English-speaking presbytery of Malaysia. We met Micky Kua above and heard about his ministry in Cornerstone Doulos Church in Petaling Jaya. Elder Phua of the Chinese church had several fine Christian children. Paul Phua is very involved in a church in Singapore. Lucy Phua has had a strategic prayer ministry and served as prayer secretary to the English-speaking presbytery. She is married to Johnson Chua, who heads up the work of Open Doors in Malaysia. We shall meet Phua Seng Tiong, in his visionary work in Sungai Way-Subang Methodist Church, later in this chapter. The other Chinese elder had a gifted young son, Tan Piah, who is vicar of the flourishing St Hilda's Church, Singapore. This church runs a Christian school with a thousand pupils which has an effective outreach into the community.

Grace Presbyterian Church has been without a minister for a few years now but the senior elder, Lim Aik Leong, who was also mentored by the OMF missionaries all those years ago, ably leads it.

One of the strengths of the English-medium churches in Johor was that they were open to all Christians. Denominational labels meant little to them. The adult leadership in Muar English Presbyterian Church consisted of a happy medley from different backgrounds. Dr Moses Tay, the leader, was an Anglican, his wife Saw Ai was Methodist,[107] Mrs Eapen came from a Mar Thoma church and Gerald and Loretta Dykema, the missionaries, were Baptist. The exporting of western denominational traditions had not helped the newly emerging churches. But somehow they often managed to overcome these divisions.

Unexpected opportunities

Another advantage of working in English was the possibility of relating to the large Gurkha garrison based on the edge of the town of Kluang. A small group of committed Gurkha Christians began to come to Martin for Bible study and prayer. This encouraged them in a situation where their faith was strongly opposed. Not only did their Hindu comrades deride their beliefs, but one day the British commanding officer challenged them on the parade ground. He had heard that several men had begun to profess the Christian faith. After a virulent attack on Christianity, he demanded, 'Anyone who is considering becoming a Christian show yourself and take one step forward.'

The whole garrison froze. Would anyone dare to stand against the commanding officer? Just one private courageously stepped forward. When the officer had finished delivering a withering rebuke, the soldier quietly replied, 'Sir, I think perhaps you do not understand the Christian faith. If you wish to know more, I will gladly explain it to you.'

That evening the commanding officer visited the soldier in his barrack room. He admitted his ignorance and asked to know more.

The dedication, courage and discipline of the Gurkha soldiers impressed Martin and me deeply. Their total devotion sometimes took us aback. On their first visit to our home I served cold drinks to everyone. In the Malaysian way, Martin invited them to drink and began to raise his glass. Their leader replied, 'Well, *we* will pray first!' While Martin held his glass they prayed a lengthy grace. We had much to learn.

One of these Gurkha Christians bought a large roll of pictures illustrating New Testament stories from us. Before we could get the picture roll to him he was transferred to East Malaysia. Amazingly, the army put his picture roll on a helicopter and flew it out to him in the jungle of Sarawak. He used the attractive pictures effectively in evangelism and teaching among the Kelabit people, and he was excited to lead several of them to believe in Christ. Ten years later a revival swept through the area and spread widely both in Sarawak and into Sabah.

Story-telling

One of Martin's problems when we lived in Kluang was
that he had little to do in the daytime as all our church
members were in school. He could not visit their homes
as their families only spoke Chinese or Indian languages. He quickly gained invitations to conferences
and other English-speaking ministries around Malaysia
and lectured one day a week at Singapore Bible College,
but still he had time on his hands.

Having worked as a hospital evangelist in South
Thailand, it seemed natural to visit in our local government hospital. Here he could use his Indonesian, a close
dialect of Malay. Malays loved to listen to him, as they
considered Indonesian to be more refined than their own
language. They would follow him, like the Pied Piper,
from ward to ward, listening to the message of Christ.
Going from bed to bed, Martin would give each patient
from the variety of racial groups a Christian gospel or
tract in their own language. These were eagerly snapped
up, as people were fascinated by the Bible stories.

While praying over this ministry he was reminded of
a comment made by Gordon Gray, a brilliant Canadian
doctor in South Thailand. Walking under the sloping
palm trees on the local tropical beach, he had observed
to Martin, 'The way to reach people here is through
story telling.' As a result, there in South Thailand Martin
had tentatively begun to tell Asianized forms of Dr Paul
White's *Jungle Doctor Stories*. To his surprise he had
found he could hold a crowd of many hundreds for an
hour in the open air, teaching biblical principles in a way
that people enjoyed and remembered.

Now in Kluang he revived his storytelling, adapting
New Testament parables to a Malaysian context. Riding
in a taxi down to Singapore each week, along with three

other passengers, Martin would launch into a story. 'Have you heard what happened to . . .?' he would begin. Catching their natural human curiosity for gossip, Martin would recount one of our Lord's parables as if set in a Malaysian scene. With much banter and discussion, interest would be aroused.

Many who listened to his stories began to examine their own religious motives. How could they change their attitudes and basic purpose in life? Might it be possible to gain a living relationship with almighty God? Was sin merely outward actions, or did it consist of something much deeper within a person's heart? Stories and parables can reach across all ethnic divides and start a spiritual hunger.

Pastor Phua Seng Tiong of the Sungai Way-Subang Methodist Church was another former member of the Batu Pahat Youth Fellowship with whom I was able to speak.

◆   ◆   ◆   ◆

Pastor Phua Seng Tiong

Pastor Phua strode purposefully ahead of Mong and me to show us his church building. He had a thin, slight frame, with black hair combed neatly back, and a fine moustache adorned his upper lip.

'This is our main auditorium,' he explained in his low quiet voice as he opened the door. I gasped. It was the size of a huge warehouse. They were obviously making provision for many hundreds of people.

'Recently we held a banquet for six hundred here,' he went on. 'It was an Honour your Father and Mother Banquet. It's very appropriate for our Chinese culture. It was a great way to share the gospel. And we are so grateful to the Lord – 30 people made a profession of faith that night.'

I glanced at the grand piano on the wide stage, the state-of-the-art PA system, full stage lighting, and all the instruments for a band. Pastor Phua added, 'Yes, we hold concerts here too. The local folk pack in. But our main purpose is really to worship the Lord and celebrate his amazing love for us. We made the room this size so it could be multi-purpose. We don't believe in separating sacred from secular – it's all God's world.'

Walking energetically ahead of us he led us to the kindergarten rooms, which they had recently built on to the side of the church. I watched him as he greeted many of the parents waiting to pick up their children and gave a small child a hug while asking how he was. The pastor was obviously well loved. As soon as his face appeared in a classroom door, the well-behaved little children chorused, 'Good morning, Pastor,' and flashed bright smiles at him.

'We care for 180 kindergarten children,' he explained. 'Chinese, Indian, Malay – they all like to come. As it's a very poor area we give some of them a subsidy. I'll show you a photo of what the area was like before we came here. Squatter houses along the river. Rubbish dumped everywhere. No pavements. No street lighting. Potholed roads. Actually we never planned to come here, it looked so God-forsaken. We've moved our venue six times as our numbers increased. When the Lord brought this plot to our attention I had less faith than my leaders. But the Lord had told us to bless this kampong (local community), especially the less fortunate, and since we came it has much improved. Even the government has now spent money on the roads.

'We aim at building relationships into the community,' he continued. 'They can't learn about the love of

Christ unless they see it in our lives. At first a particular fundamentalist sect in the kampong objected strongly to our presence. All we could do was pray – and didn't we pray – asking God to cause confusion on our opponents while the building work began. Then without our doing anything, suddenly the government rounded up all the extremists nationwide, imprisoning the leaders and disbanding the rest. It was such an answer to prayer!

'Actually it's very tough here spiritually. There are Indians with their temples and shrines, and Chinese and Indonesians with all their superstitions. We just have to rely on prayer and go forward.'

Glancing at my fair skin Pastor Phua asked, 'Are you happy to walk in the heat? I'd like to show you our two shoplot buildings.' I assured him I was fine and he led the way down a couple of streets. 'We've bought these three houses for our Chinese-speaking ministry as many of our members have friends or elderly parents who are Chinese-speaking. But we also use the premises during the week for tuition and community outreach. English, maths and computer studies are the main subjects some of our young volunteers and retired members offer. And also downstairs is a woodwork vocational centre. Children come from all the different ethnic groups and it's a wonderful way to break down their initial suspicion of having Christians in their neighbourhood.'

Back at the church we crossed the basketball court and Pastor Phua also mentioned the street soccer pitch they had made on the nearby car park. 'Every evening many young people and children come to play or to watch. It gives us a golden opportunity to mingle and to build bridges,' he explained.

We were back in the small office near the front door as Pastor Phua continued. 'When we were erecting this present church, the building contractor was converted too. He wanted to set up a Taoist shrine before starting, but we forbade him.

'How can my workmen be kept safe?' he demanded. 'Building can be very dangerous work.' But I assured him that we would pray. We had people praying on site with fasting and half-nights of prayer. And the workers who were non-believers were kept free from accidents. In fact we saw many other miracles. There was one time when they had to work until seven o'clock but dark storm clouds had gathered over the building site. The workers got ready to stop even though it was only four o'clock. Some of us who were at the site gathered together to pray, and miraculously we saw the Lord literally cause the clouds to be blown away before our very eyes.

"That can't possibly be due to your prayer," the contractor expostulated. But God did it again for us – stopped another downpour. It was amazing!'

I agreed that was a gracious answer to prayer indeed. 'But tell me,' I asked him, 'how did your church start originally and how were you yourself converted?'

'It's a long story,' he answered quietly. 'I'm a third-generation Christian. My grandmother was converted in China and led her husband to the Lord. I was told that she often spoke about the China Inland Mission so I presume she had links with them. They emigrated to Malaya and attended the Chinese Presbyterian Church in Batu Pahat, Johor.'

'Oh, these last few days I've met others from the English youth group in Batu Pahat!' I exclaimed.

'Yes, a number of us have gone into full-time ministry. OMF came at a time when a change was needed in Batu Pahat. The Chinese section got their pastors from China but they tended to be traditional and rather liberal. Dr Timothy Tow from Singapore used to visit us in the English section. He was a gifted speaker and was more

evangelical, but he tended to be separatist. When the
OMF missionaries came, they showed us that this was
not the only stand we could take. They taught us that
even though we were evangelical we need not be exclu-
sive, but we could welcome people from many different
kinds of churches as long as they loved the Lord.

'At that time OMF was experiencing a shift in policy and realizing that they should not be holed up
exclusively in the New Villages. Effective work could
also be done through the existing churches. So we in
Batu Pahat benefited from this new attitude. I learned
so much from Ryland-Jones. His teaching was a bit
over the heads of the school kids, but I was attending
university by then and he really stretched me. He was
more a trainer than a pastor.

'Peter Warner was great, too. He inspired many
young people to go into full-time ministry. He and
Ronalda were so warm and welcoming and kept an
open home for us younger people. I was in a quandary
about what to do with my life when I graduated. I'd
been refused teacher training college even though I had
the necessary grades. So Peter challenged me to apply to
a Bible school in Australia. I was about to go when, out
of the blue, a telegram came saying I could go for teacher
training, and I felt that was the right step. But God had
planted seeds concerning mission in my heart and I
never forgot it.'

'So you worked as a teacher all your life?' I asked.

'Yes, for 31 years, and as a school principal as well.
Actually I came to join the Methodist church by default,'
he added with a laugh. 'There was no Presbyterian church
nearby in Petaling Jaya when I studied at the university. I
tried the Brethren, and that was a culture shock: I could
not get used to the silences. The Baptists wouldn't have
me, as I hadn't been baptized by immersion. But there

was need for a Sunday School teacher in Trinity
Methodist Church. An OMF speaker had said to us students, "Wherever you are you need to serve. Always look
for a niche where you can serve the Lord." So I joined the
Methodists, even though they weren't very evangelical.

'Some concerned evangelical Methodists started the
Aldersgate[108] Prayer Fellowship about that time. It must
have been 1970. Their aim was to bring revival back to
the Methodist church, feeling that we must get back to
the Bible and strengthen our roots. This brought blessing
to many and several began to pray about going into
Christian ministry.

'At that time we also realized that there were many
church members living in our area who were not going
to church. So a group of us started a preaching point.
This was thirty years ago. An American Methodist pastor was happy to lead us, but he had to return to the USA
after six or eight months, leaving us with a free hand. We
were very radical, all being young graduates together,
and several of us were influenced by OMF. For example
there was Peter Sze, who had worked with Mary
Welander in Segamat and Amarasingam, who had links
with OMF in Penang and became the first and only
Malaysian on the joint Singapore-Malaysia Home
Council. Having been mentored by missionaries, our
aim was that mission should be our way of life.
Remembering their simple lifestyle and willingness to
persevere, we too wanted to give our all to extending
God's kingdom.

'So we were very bold. As a new and young church
we decided that for every dollar that the church received
we would give away 51 cents! And the Lord has kept us
to this all these thirty years since we started. Sixty per
cent of our receipts now goes to mission.'

'How do you do it?' I asked him.

'I don't really know,' Pastor Phua replied. 'But when you make a covenant with the Lord he always gives a surplus. You might say: God has given us a gift of generosity. We have approximately five hundred members now, and every year we hold a gift day for mission, over and above our normal budget. We set a target: $3,000 was the goal in 1976 when we started. It felt like a lot then, but God helped us. This year our target was $1 million, and the Lord gave us $1.15 million. I say it with a great sense of humility and faith, because it is God who does it each time.'

That amazing gift day seemed a miracle enough, but Pastor Phua had more to share with us.

'At present we have six long-term missionaries: a guy in Bolivia, a lady in Hong Kong, a couple in Indonesia and my son and his wife who have just joined the OM ship. But we encourage all our members to go on short-term trips – about 150 go each year. Recently whole families have been going, so the children too can experience mission. We are linked with work in Myanmar, India, Bangladesh, Cambodia, Vietnam, Laos, Thailand and Indonesia. And we have also sent people to Pakistan, Mongolia and Israel.'

'What an organization!' I thought to myself. 'One hundred and fifty people going on short-term trips, all needing to be briefed and the travel plans worked out. And what a list of countries.' But before I could comment Pastor Phua continued.

'Then of course there's our local outreach, running the kindergarten – all our teachers are Christian and look for opportunities to witness. The children's church is bursting at the seams and has more than a hundred volunteers to run it. And we have family camps each year and open house at Christmas when we invite our friends from the kampong to join us for a night of food and fellowship.'

My head was spinning by this stage. What a vision for mission. 'The Malaysians have taken over from us and they are doing it ten times better!' I thought. How wonderfully God works. But this was not all.

'I ought to mention, too, that God has led us into church-planting training courses in Cambodia,' Pastor Phua continued. 'After the horrendous atrocities there the people are wide open to the gospel. For seven years now we have sent teams to Phnom Penh, training Cambodians to plant churches. The local pastors select 30 people to come for three months of training and then they go out to evangelize. We weren't very skilled the first two years, but after that we refined the course. These Cambodian church planters have now planted over two hundred churches. We help them financially the first year and then they are on their own. And the course is now 60 per cent taught by Cambodian Christians, because they are growing spirit-ually and becoming more competent.'

And still he hadn't finished.

'Then there are the Cambodian maids,' he went on. 'Many come over here to earn money and send it home. God has a strange way of doing things sometimes. One of our members runs an employment agency for these maids. Because our church has so many connections over there this member goes to the villages and selects perhaps a hundred young women. They are given a three or four month training before they come, so they will know what to expect and how to handle things. During that time, of course, they hear about the Lord and most of them become Christians. When they start work in Malaysia our church member tells their employers that these are Christian maids and please may they have time off on Sundays to come to church. Then we pick them up in the van and bring them to a service. We run services in Chinese and the national language and Cambodian as well as our main English services.'

As we said our farewells and expressed our gratitude for all the time Pastor Phua had given us, Mong and I thanked God for pouring out his grace in such a remarkable way. Here were a few young graduates who had dedicated themselves wholly to the Lord and who are reaping an amazing harvest for God today. Pastor Phua was so obviously in love with the Lord that it shone in his face as he spoke to us. What a challenge he and his team of voluntary workers present. He epitomized for me a man who could say, 'For me, to live is Christ!' (Phil. 1:21).[109]

15.

Malaysians Are the Missionaries of Today

It has been an amazing privilege to meet so many Malaysian Christians and to marvel at what God has done over the last 50 years. I have only seen a fraction of what is happening today, and I have only been able to learn about a tiny portion of what has taken place over the years. But one thing has become clear. The churches of Asia are experiencing a remarkable work of God. Whereas they used to be 'receiving' churches (largely dependent on the West for their evangelism, teaching and growth) now they have become fully 'sending' churches (able not only to stand on their own feet but also to play an increasingly significant part in the evangelism of Asia and indeed of the world).

This forms part of the momentous shift which has taken place in the history of the worldwide church in the second half of the twentieth century. While churches in Europe appear to be shrinking due to many factors, including the tragedies of two world wars and the spread of post-modernism, churches in Asia, Latin America and Africa show striking growth. Today there are more practising Lutherans in Indonesia than in

Germany, more Baptists and Pentecostals in Brazil than in Western Europe, and more practising Anglicans in Nigeria alone than in the United Kingdom, Canada, United States, New Zealand and Australia put together. Likewise there are more active Presbyterians in South Korea, as also in Indonesia, than in all of Europe.[110]

By the power of the Holy Spirit, many of the so-called 'younger' churches now form vibrant witnessing communities, reaching out into their neighbourhoods and beyond with attractive effectiveness. The churches of Malaysia fully bear this out. In spite of the discouragingly slow beginnings 150 years ago, and then the huge odds stacked against them when our story began after the Second World War, God has demonstrated again his ability to work miracles in answer to his servants' sacrifice and prayers.

Many of those whose lives were touched by the missionaries are now serving God in all walks of life. In Malaysia today Christian doctors model their practices on our Lord's life of healing and service. Christian nurses and dentists and paramedics are motivated in their profession by this same pattern which our Lord set. Christian business people and lawyers are seeking to transform society by biblical values. Christian teachers are prayerfully impacting the young lives around them for the kingdom of God. Christian social workers and carers have pioneered establishments for the care of the underprivileged, opening the eyes of the government and the local authorities to the worth of these often slighted individuals. Each one could tell a story of how God is using them to build up his church in Malaysia and to demonstrate the glories of the revelation which God has given us in Christ.

And as we have seen also, the churches of Malaysia are sending out their members in short-term and long-term mission to other countries.

One who heard the call of God to leave her homeland and get involved in international mission first heard the gospel when she was only two or three years old in the New Village of Rasa, Selangor State. Rasa was the village which Martin visited briefly as a new missionary, where he received looks of animosity as he made his way to the home of the resident missionaries that he never forgot. It was nicknamed Little Moscow because of its strong Communist ties. Yet little Yit Meng, later called Rachel, was living in Rasa and felt drawn to the Saviour at a very early age. When she was about eleven, Keith Ranger held an evangelistic meeting near Rachel's father's coffee shop and she was drawn to listen to the songs he played on his piano accordion.

Soon after that, a white man with white hair came visiting house to house and invited Rachel and her sister to a home meeting in the tailor's shop each Friday night. Later Rachel discovered that his name was Stanley Rowe, or Uncle Stanley as he became known to all her friends. She was too shy to go at first, and when Stanley Rowe started a meeting at her school she would stand outside, listening to the singing and hoping someone would notice her and invite her in. She felt drawn like a magnet to these meetings although she did not know why.

Not long afterwards, an Indian doctor organized a youth camp where Uncle Stanley gave the Bible studies, and there Rachel finally understood what Jesus had done for her. The tears coursed down her face as she prayed the sinner's prayer.

Rachel found her life was changed. She and her friends used to gamble their money; in fact, she even stole so she'd have money for gambling. But gambling completely lost its grip on her. She also loved basketball and was a member of the local team. But when they changed their practice time from Wednesday to Friday she gave that up too because the time clashed with the youth meeting.

Uncle Stanley lovingly mentored her and encouraged her to come to all the meetings. He would give her copies of the *Soon* magazine, produced by the World Evangelisation Crusade (WEC), and she would devour them faster than he could get new ones. He also gave her the *Upward Path Bible* correspondence course, as she was really hungry for God's truth.

When she moved to the Victoria Institution in Kuala Lumpur for her 'A' levels, Rachel had an experience which was to change her life. A team from the *MV Logos* ship came to talk at her school and at her church (Jalan Imbi Chapel) and she was very challenged by their work and started to pray for missions. Because she knew little about missions except what she had learnt from Uncle Stanley, she went to the OMF Centre in Jalan Ampang to ask for more information. Unfortunately, whoever she spoke to gave her a thick volume called *The Principles and Practices of OMF*, which completely put her off! So she presumed that she was not a suitable candidate.

God's plan, however, was not thwarted by this unthinking action. Some years later, after Rachel graduated in computer studies and successfully climbed the promotion ladder of a quasi-government firm, the Lord spoke clearly to her. She was to join Operation Mobilisation (OM), not OMF! His directions to her were so unmistakable she knew she must obey. At the time she was walking on a lovely beach on the island of Phuket. The scene was beautiful and serene, but her heart was in turmoil, especially as she was a few months away from a promotion which would make her supervisor of a pilot project in Sabah, with a corresponding rise in salary.

Her boss almost fell out of his chair when she handed in her resignation. 'Leave your religious duties until you reach retirement,' he urged her over a private lunch together. From his Asian viewpoint he was implying, 'Get the best out of your life and leave the leftover to God – he won't mind!' But Rachel had no peace until she took the decisive step to resign. All the 'what ifs' flooded her mind. She had never done anything like this before, and she had never been without a steady source of income, and it was scary.

When OM accepted her application for a two-year service, Rachel had no financial backing from anywhere and did not have enough money even for the initial conference. She told me. 'That experience was like taking a leap in the dark, but it was exhilarating, and just when I felt like I was falling into the bottomless unknown, God's hand caught hold of me.' Just two days before she boarded the plane for Europe, the necessary money came in.

After the initial summer crusade she had the joy of joining Uncle Stanley, who was now working in Amsterdam. Together they visited many Chinese restaurants. 'Always carry tracts with you wherever you go,' he'd urged her. Rachel learned so much from his passion for the Chinese and from watching him at work. Listening to him preach about love in the wee hours of the morning after the restaurants had closed, she thought to herself, 'This is love, that this man is willing to sacrifice sleep in order to reach the lost for Christ.'

God has brought Rachel a long way. Later she worked with Ethel Barkworth in Peter Young's CARE Centre and her heart was touched to reach out to the handicapped and people abandoned by their families. After studying at the WEC training school in Tasmania she served with the same organization in Pakistan for four eventful years. Then she had the unexpected joy of meeting an old friend from the *MV Logos* days. Lindsay Flintoff fell in love with her. They married and she has been serving with him as a WEC missionary in Thailand since 1989.

Rachel Flintoff had the privilege of seeing Stanley Rowe just nine days before the Lord took him into his presence. She always felt he was the one who had the most impact on her life for God.

At the Keswick Convention in 1998 she bumped into Keith and Catherine Ranger and realized that he must have been the accordion-playing missionary who came to Rasa all those years ago. It gave her confidence to know that the seeds she was busy sowing among children in Thailand would yield results by God's grace and faithfulness. She exclaimed, 'I can't wait to see who else will be there to surprise me around the throne of grace, on the other shore one day.'

Rachel is one example of many Malaysians who have offered their lives to God for cross-cultural missionary work.

Having spent almost a hundred years of its earlier ministry in China, OMF was regrettably slow in welcoming Asians as full members of its Caucasian mission. In the middle of the last century lines were firmly drawn in many people's minds between 'mission sending countries' and 'the mission field'. Asia remained 'the mission field'. An unconscious paternalism still gripped the minds of many mission leaders.

Martin remembers a gifted young lady in his Bible class in 1960 who felt strongly called by God to serve as a missionary. But OMF was not yet ready to open its doors to her, and she could find no Asian mission to join. Disillusioned and disappointed, some years later she abandoned her Christian faith.

But 1965 brought the centenary of OMF, and with it came a challenge to fresh thinking and ideas. One of these was to open the membership to anyone from any nationality – a radical step at that time. New possibilities flashed across the scene as suddenly narrow horizons began to broaden. I attended OMF's first mission conference for Asians and remember meeting there an African visitor who was passing through. Amazed at seeing so many Chinese Christians he exclaimed, 'In my country the only Chinese we meet are Communists. I had no idea there were so many Chinese Christians.'

His reaction underlined the challenge to the participants that there was a great world out there waiting to hear the good news of Jesus Christ. And Chinese Christians could be part of the answer.

Gradually OMF set up home councils in each of their fields of operation. So after the political separation from Singapore, the Malaysian Home Council was formed in 1978 under the godly leadership of Dr David Gunaratnam. He served as their dedicated and able chairman for 24 years.

Stella Hooi, who was a leading light in the Malaysian Nurses Christian Fellowship, was the first Malaysian missionary to be accepted to join OMF. She came from a Christian family in Penang and was a gentle, caring person, always ready to listen to anyone in need. She served at first in Manorom Christian Hospital, Thailand, and then in Nongbua Christian Hospital, and was well loved among the Thai. Even after having to resign in 1987 in order to nurse her father, she continued her spiritual ministry. Today Stella is still active and prayerful among doctors and nurses.

Other candidates also applied, like Koh Leng Kue, with her bright personality and obvious gifts to make an impact for God. She also served in Thailand, in the south of the country. More missionaries followed, ministering in a wide variety of countries. Choo Yew On and his wife

Chern Chern, for example, are skilled orthodontists who lecture in the University of Phnom Penh and have wide opportunities for Christian witness. Tan Yu Keong, with his legal training, and Li Min, a trained accountant, are serving their Lord in the distant city of Urumqui in north west China. Sereen Koh has been using her nursing skills as she works in a squatters' church in Hong Kong. And Koh Guat Lian works near her as the area secretary for OMF in Hong Kong. Liew Tong Ngan and his wife Yoshie have taken up the challenge of student ministry as missions secretary to the International Fellowship of Evangelical Students. They have been involved in the exciting work of training, networking and recruiting people to work in the universities of East Asia.

Today there are more than 20 Malaysian members of OMF working in Thailand, China, Cambodia, Hong Kong and Macau. In addition, another ten have cross-cultural marriages and are sent out from USA, UK and other countries. These people serve in Mongolia, the Philippines, Taiwan and China. Dr Alex Matthews, a leading Indian Christian in Kuala Lumpur, took up the leadership of the team in 2002. In God's grace, all the missionaries sent by the Malaysian Home Council since the 1980s are still serving today. In all these years there have been no losses or casualties. This is particularly significant when the average period of missionary service from all countries worldwide is less than six years.

Heading up this work as the newly appointed Malaysian Home Director is my wonderful friend, Mong, with whom I had the joy of conducting many of the interviews incorporated in this book. I listened to her story as I lay in bed in the Methodist Centre in Malaka, recovering from a tummy upset. It is truly amazing how God has led her and how she was prepared in strange ways for a great task.

◆   ◆   ◆   ◆

Yap Heong Mong

Mong found herself lying on a trolley, waiting for an emergency operation in a hospital in England. Her face was horribly lacerated by the shattering of her glasses in a car accident. All round her face and lips were cuts, requiring at least 50 stitches. Her right hand had suffered such a deep wound that if she had been cut a fraction more she would have lost the use of it entirely. Her two legs would have been broken except that her tall strong leather boots protected them.

'God, what's happening?' she groaned. 'Please help me to be attended to quickly!' But it was nine long hours before she was finally wheeled into the operating theatre at 7 o'clock that night. But at exactly that time her Christian friends in Bedford, 35 miles away, started their prayer meeting. News of Mong's accident had come to them and they prayed fervently for the surgeon's skill and her healing. A month later the surgeon expressed his amazement at the completeness of her recovery. She did not need the plastic surgery he had anticipated.

Only a few Sundays before, Mong had been at a service in their Baptist church, listening to a sermon on Isaiah 6. The challenge had been given in the words of God himself. 'Whom shall I send and who will go for us?' Doubting her own adequacy, Mong had replied in her heart, 'Not me, Lord! I'll earn money for missions. Send someone else.'

And now here she lay, slowly recovering, while God's challenge rang in her ears. Her friends from the Baptist church and others in the Chinese Christian fellowship plied her with flowers, visiting her and praying for her, and loving her back to strength. Slowly Mong began to realize that God had spared her for a purpose, and gradually she became willing to obey God – whatever he asked of her.

Some time before her accident, while studying accountancy, Mong had become a Christian through the ministry of the Chinese Overseas Christian Mission. She was the only Asian working in her accountancy firm in Bedford, UK, and the other staff had jeered at her when she told them she wanted to be baptized. And now this tragic accident had maimed her face – a woman's pride and joy. Her colleagues urged her to take the driver of the car to court. It was clearly his fault. But Mong could not retaliate in this way and left the situation in God's hands. Lying in bed, she felt the love of God in such an amazing way that it flooded her heart. 'OK God,' she whispered at last. 'Anywhere, any time. I'll do what you want.'

Later, commissioned by Denmark Street Baptist Church in Bedford to return to Malaysia, she faced another crisis point as an offer for marriage came. But the Lord reminded her of her call to mission and painfully she made her decision to refuse the proposal. Her suitor found this very difficult to accept, and Mong's family and friends could not understand her reasons. But God spoke into her heart, reassuring her and telling her to be at peace over the decision. He had greater things in store for her.

On her return to her homeland, OMF asked Mong to join the home council, but within weeks she felt under strong attack. Her father died suddenly from a stroke and then, six months later, her mother also died from a stroke. While she was still reeling from the grief of her double bereavement, three months later her fourth brother's wife died suddenly, leaving behind three small children, aged three and a half, 21 months and two months.

'God, what are you doing?' she gasped, as the care of the three children fell into her lap and the paternal grandmother, who was in her eighties, also needed her care. A final straw appeared to be the family business going bankrupt a few months later. 'How can I get through all this?' Mong asked herself as she worked full-time as an accountant while supporting her brother with his traumatized children. Again God drew close to her, this time through the words of Isaiah 43:2

> *When you pass through the waters, I will be with you; and when you pass through the rivers, they will not sweep over you. When you walk through the fire, you will not be burned.*

With her heavy family responsibilities Mong's commitment to mission never left her. God was honing her and teaching her – not through a Bible college as had been her desire, but through the severe testing of family responsibilities and bereavement. As government restrictions hindered new expatriate OMFers from coming to Malaysia, more and more of those who were present had to leave under the ten-year rule.

With her role on the OMF Malaysian home council and feeling discouraged at the desperate shortage of workers, Mong asked the Lord again, 'God, what are you doing? How can the church in Malaysia grow without the missionaries' help?' This time she felt an audible voice, 'What about you? It's time for you to join OMF.' Horrified at the thought, she felt so scared that she dared not read her Bible in case God spoke to her again. Then she repented and asked for a sign, 'If you really want me as a missionary, dear Lord, please may OMF approach me themselves.'

By God's wonderful grace, at that very moment Dr David Gunaratnam, the Malaysian council chairman,

was discussing Mong's gifting and situation with Dr
James Taylor, great-grandson of the founder of the China
Inland Mission and at that time General Director of
OMF. They both felt it right to offer Mong the role of
executive secretary for the Malaysian Home Council.
She was so amazed she could not sleep that night, but
she knew she had to accept.

But how could she tell her boss at work? She prayed
hard and approached him. But before she could say anything, he announced that he needed to talk with her.
Government directives were forcing him to appoint a
Malay accountant as head of the firm, and this made it
very easy for Mong to hand in her resignation.

Mong has now served for 20 years as a highly valued
Malaysian member of OMF. Her gifts in accountancy
have been used to the full, both in two tours in Hong
Kong and then at the International Headquarters as
Director of Finance for the whole mission, an extremely
important task. She held this role while they were completely revising their financial policy and the complica-
tions involved reverberated throughout the mission.

While she was in Hong Kong, her organizational skills
were used to upgrade the structures and efficiency of
OMF's rapidly expanding work into China, and travel to
that country has greatly enriched her. During these years
she has developed lovely gifts of relating to others with
deep insight and encouragement. She has been happy to
lead or to play second fiddle as the situation demanded,
willingly dovetailing her gifts with the gifts of others. Her
responsibilities to her brother's growing children have
also taken up much of her time. Teenagers without a
mother can feel very hurt and resentful, so over the years
Mong has poured love and acceptance into their lives.

Recently she has been appointed the Home Director
of OMF Malaysia, with responsibility for any expatriate

missionaries as well as the larger task of recruiting, sending out and caring for Malaysians joining OMF. God has
prepared her in many unexpected ways for this task,
even though again and again she has felt inadequate.
But the Lord has reassured her with Jesus' words, 'You
did not choose me, but I chose you and appointed you to
go and bear fruit – fruit that will last' (Jn. 15:16).[111]

Epilogue

Forty years on

'I wonder what Vergis Matthew will be like now,' I said to my husband as our plane touched down in Kuala Lumpur.

When we pastored the English-speaking Presbyterian church in Kluang in the mid-1960s, Vergis was a good-looking, lanky teenager and a faithful member of our youth group. His family were Malayali, linked to the ancient churches probably founded by the Apostle Thomas within a few decades of our Lord's resurrection. Vergis had emailed us when he heard that we were to speak to the OMF Malaysia conference in 2003, and he invited us to pay a return visit to Kluang after all these years.

Instead of the lanky teenager, the man who greeted us at the airport barrier was a successful, grey-haired and distinguished-looking accountant who used his mobile phone to bring the car to the exit.

'What a lot has changed in the past 40 years!' I thought as I settled into the comfortable back seat. We had no mobile phones back then, and very few of our friends in Kluang would have owned a car. We saw signs already of how Malaysia had prospered economically since the 1960s. But this was just the beginning.

As we sped south along the wide smooth dual carriageway in air-conditioned comfort we vividly remembered long, hot journeys in our little Morris traveller, stuck behind huge timber lorries, plying our two toddlers with drinks to keep them cool. It used to take us almost a whole day to travel from Kluang to Kuala Lumpur. That day we reached our destination in only a few hours.

Vergis filled us in with news of our old friends. Most of them had been teenagers when we knew them, because the English congregation had begun as a children's meeting. Hardly any adults attended at that time, as only a few older people were fluent enough in English to be able to worship comfortably in that language. The youthfulness of the rest of the congregation had made any older people hesitant to join us.

Today the church is filled with whole families: grandparents, parents and children, and the membership has grown to several hundred.

'We are planning to erect our own building,' Vergis continued. 'It's been great being able to share the Chinese-speaking congregation's church, but we often find we want to hold a meeting just when they've planned to use it. And of course they have first preference. The government doesn't easily give permission to build a new church, and so it has taken us six years of prayer and petitioning before it came. Now we really praise God that it has been granted. We'll take you to see where the foundations are being excavated. We're all very excited about it!'

As we reached the town of Kluang we were amazed at the change which had taken place. Far from being the rather sleepy market town we remembered, it now formed a central part of Malaysia's Silicon Valley. The streets were full of modern shops and smart restaurants. The housing estates extended far beyond what we could remember, so that we found it difficult to orientate ourselves. Our old home, which used to lie down a twisting small side road, seemed to have completely disappeared. Unlike the cement floor and slatted wooden walls we had been used to, the modern houses looked substantial and beautifully built. I had been dreading being in the tropical heat again, as I had memories of pushing my two small children in an unsprung carrycot to visit church members while the perspiration rolled down my back. But now air-conditioning was common everywhere and I need not have feared the heat.

Martin and I were overwhelmed at the welcome the church gave us. Although there had been a number of other missionaries before we came, Martin was their first pastor and so they remembered us with special love. A reunion dinner had been carefully planned to which nearly a hundred people came, some travelling from Singapore and further afield. It was wonderful to meet those who had been in the church as young people and to see, after 40 years, how they had grown and blossomed. Now they were mature and respected Christian leaders.

When we were in Kluang the church started a weekly offering, quite a new venture for them. This helped to cover our rent. Then as gifts came in later and the church could afford it, Malaysian pastors took over from the missionaries and the whole church life flourished much more under their care. We were struck by the spiritual maturity of men and women alike, and by their keenness to learn and to grow. Questions flowed about all aspects of the Christian life, not only there in the restaurant over our reunion dinner. Several wanted to come to the house where we were staying the next day in their eagerness for all they could imbibe. There was a spiritual dynamic and an uninhibited hunger for holiness and Christ-likeness which we longed to see in our own church in Britain.

One particular joy was to renew friendship with Teo Eng Lin, now a lovely matriarch in the church, gifted in organizing and uninhibited in making her opinions known. How well we remembered her lovely smile and charming dimple! She first heard the gospel many years ago in England while doing her teacher training. Friends had taken her to church there, but she thought, 'These are all white people here. Christianity is not for the Chinese.' To her amazement, when she returned home she met some *Chinese* Christians, and this opened her eyes. 'Might Chinese too follow this new faith?' she wondered, and so she began to explore the possibility.

It had not been easy when she first declared her allegiance to Christ. Her home was strongly idolatrous and every day all the food except the rice was placed on the ancestral spirit shelf before being brought to the table. As her mother refused her request for some of the dishes not to be offered in this way, out of loyalty to Christ she ate nothing but rice and ketchup for six months – such had been her strong determination to follow her Lord whatever it cost.

Teo Eng Lin's father had married five wives. When we knew her, one of the wives and her father had died. We have vivid memories of visiting her home. The clickety-click of mah-jong filled the house as the four wives spent all day gambling. And the smell of smoking joss sticks filled the air. One of her mothers practised as a spirit medium and the oppressive darkness could almost be felt. But Eng Lin became one of our closest friends. Aged at that time in her late twenties, she proved a wise member of the church committee, always having something useful to contribute.

Under strong and able leadership, the new church building was completed in 18 months. And amazingly by God's grace, Martin and I were once more back in Asia in June 2005 and so we were able to attend the opening. The attractiveness of the spacious new building, the lovely seating arrangement and the beautiful displays of tropical flowers struck us. The choir had new white satin gowns with large deep crimson overlap, and a group of five young girls led the worship dance very movingly in their shimmering midnight blue and white dresses. Following the Jewish pattern, a loud blast on a ram's horn started the proceedings, and the sense of joy and celebration was palpable as the band led our singing. One after another the church leaders told how amazingly God had enabled them to erect their own church.

But one small cloud hung over the service. The authorities had been unwilling to grant a certificate of fitness which was necessary before the building could be opened. After much prayer and many visits to the office, eventually a temporary certificate was issued, only for the day of opening. Everyone thought there might still be a long delay before permission was given for permanent use of their new church. God answered these prayers, and the climax to the proceedings came when Vergis Matthew was able to announce that the permanent certificate had arrived and the church was now fully open. Loud cheers all over the hall greeted his statement, and the sense of gratitude to God for all his miracles deepened. What a privilege it was for Martin to be asked to preach on such an occasion!

The celebrations concluded with abundant refreshments as the congregation enjoyed fellowship together. Old friendships were deepened and newer members sensed the reality of Christian love in the family of God. Eating and drinking together is biblically significant and it plays a central part in every Asian culture.

What has happened in Kluang is also happening today all over west Malaysia. Up and down the country God is answering prayer. Among the Chinese and Indians, as indeed among all the peoples resident in Malaysia, many are becoming Christians. As we have seen, new church buildings are bursting at the seams, with dedicated and visionary leaders. And from what were once tiny and struggling churches the gospel is now spreading out into the surrounding nations.

'Nothing is impossible with God!' (Luke 1:37)

The words of the angel Gabriel ring out with confidence across the centuries. Again and again God has worked his miracles in situations which appeared difficult and hopeless. As we look at the story of the church in Malaysia we can echo the truth of the angel's words. We in other countries, too, can take courage for the many tough situations in the world today where the gospel is struggling against tremendous odds. God has built a living vibrant church in a country which appeared so unpromising 50 years ago, and he can do the same in other, equally daunting, situations.

We have seen how those early church planters were up against enormous problems of every kind. Physically, life was difficult in a tropical climate with no electricity, poor housing and sanitation, and debilitating illnesses. Politically, they initially found themselves in a war zone, as hated foreigners who were suspected of siding with the enemy. Socially, they were launched into a culture radically different from their own and tackling a myriad of mutually unintelligible languages. Religiously, they were called to evangelize people who held strong beliefs, handed down to them from many generations. And spiritually they were up against the blatant power of Satan and demonic forces.

But in spite of all these hindrances they persevered, in prayer, in unremitting evangelism and in discipling to build up the kingdom of God, believing there would be a harvest one day.

The material they worked with appeared unpromising to begin with, as usually only the children and young people would gather. For years the churches appeared weak, with few natural leaders emerging. But through focussing on the ones whose hearts God opened, training them up, taking them along on evangelistic mission, and giving them increasing responsibility, gradually autonomous churches arose – and then the church really began to multiply under national leadership.

Extending the kingdom of God is no easy task. Many Christians today are up against equally daunting challenges as they long and pray to see God work. In western Europe, as also in many countries where Islam or Buddhism holds sway, evangelistic mission can seem discouraging and slow. But we need to remember that all major movements of God started from tough situations.

May this story fill us all with a fresh confidence in the God of the impossible. May each one of us stick to our calling, expecting the Holy Spirit to break through with power and build his church. We can be sure that God is with us, just as he was with the growing church in Malaysia. And whether we live to see it or not, may the church of Christ world-wide grow and blossom until the whole earth is *'filled with the knowledge of the glory of the Lord, as the waters cover the sea'* (Hab. 2:14).

Endnotes

1. Mary Welander, 'The Time to Tell' (unpublished).
2. Shy, but imposing physically and as a personality and speaker, Leslie Lyall had been involved in a revival movement among students in Beijing. He became Candidates Secretary for CIM in London, although his heart was still in Asia. He wrote various influential books on China and Chinese Christians.
3. *The Millions* (July 1952).
4. Don Fleming (personal correspondence).
5. David Bentley-Taylor, *China's Millions* (May 1951).
6. David Bentley-Taylor, *China's Millions* (July 1951).
7. Victor Purcell, *The Chinese of South-East Asia* (Oxford: OUP, 1951).
8. R. Alan Cole, *Emerging Pattern in the Diocese of Singapore and Malaya* (London: CIM, 1961).
9. Personal correspondence with Betty Laing. Betty and her fellow worker Doris Dove were the first two single lady workers of the mission to arrive in Malaya.
10. Betty Laing (personal correspondence).
11. George Williamson, an experienced CIM missionary who later became Superintendent of the CIM North Malaya Field.

12 Welander, 'The Time to Tell'.

13 This new worker was Peter Murray, the son of CIM missionaries, who in the aftermath of the war was left in Shanghai where he worked as a dock labourer.

14 A reminiscence from Don Fleming (personal correspondence).

15 Don Fleming (personal correspondence).

16 Cole, *Emerging Pattern*.

17 Ralph Toliver, *The Millions* (July/Aug. 1954).

18 *The Millions* (July/Aug. 1952).

19 David Bentley-Taylor, *The Millions* (Feb. 1953).

20 Nora Rowe, *The Millions* (Oct. 1952).

21 Ralph Toliver, *The Millions* (July/Aug. 1954).

22 *The Millions* (Feb. 1959).

23 Ralph Toliver.

24 Interviewed 22 June 2005.

25 A.F. Glasser, minutes of the CIM Leaders' Conference in Bournemouth 1951.

26 Bournemouth 1951.

27 Bournemouth 1951.

28 Bournemouth 1951.

29 Central Council 1954.

30 Ibid.

31 Ibid.

32 Ibid.

33 Ibid.

34 Ibid.

35 David Bentley-Taylor, *The Millions* (May 1951).

36 Welander, 'The Time to Tell', p. 5.

37 *The Millions* (Jan. 1955).

38 See David Bentley-Taylor's books *The Prisoner Leaps* (London: CIM, 1961), *Java Saga* and *The Weathercock's Reward* (London: CIM/OMF, 1967). He has also recently authored several historical biographies, e.g. on Augustine and Erasmus.

[39] *The Millions* (May 1952).

[40] *The Millions* (July/Aug. 1952).

[41] Ibid.

[42] David Bentley-Taylor, *The Millions* (Oct. 1952).

[43] *OMF Bulletin* (July 1952).

[44] Nora Rowe, *The Millions* (May 1953).

[45] Edith Cork, *The Millions* (May 1952).

[46] Winnie Rand, *The Millions* (Oct. 1952).

[47] Edith Cork, *The Millions* (Jan. 1953).

[48] Doris Madden, The Millions (Jun. 1952).

[49] This has become a major issue for Christians in Western Europe. For further reading on this topic see C. Wright, *Thinking Clearly About the Uniqueness of Jesus* (Oxford: Monarch, 1997) and M. Goldsmith, *What About Other Faiths?* (London: Hodder & Stoughton, 2002).

[50] Fern Blair (personal correspondence).

[51] *CIM Bulletin* (Nov. 1952).

[52] *CIM Bulletin* (July 1953).

[53] For further discussion of this difficult subject see M. Goldsmith, *Get a Grip on Mission* (Nottingham: IVP, 2006), ch. 9.

[54] *CIM Bulletin* (July 1953).

[55] *CIM Bulletin* (July 1954).

[56] Despite this controversy, some south Malayan missionaries continued to attend the NVCC as non-voting representatives, and the committee continued to clear their requests for work in the New Villages.

[57] At the Kuala Lumpur Baptist Church (interviewed 24 June 2005).

[58] Personal conversation.

[59] Originally in China there were several such denominational fields, but the others had lapsed after some years.

[60] *The Millions* (Jan. 1954).

[61] Ibid.

[62] Ibid.

63 A.J. Lea, *CIM Bulletin* (Mar. 1953).
64 *The Millions* (Feb. 1955).
65 Ibid.
66 *The Millions* (June 1956).
67 *The Millions* (Jan. 1956).
68 Interviewed 27 June 2005.
69 *The Millions* (Apr. 1965).
70 Ellen Lister (personal correspondence).
71 Memoirs of St Andrew's Church, Bidor (published by the Anglican Diocese of West Malaysia, 1952 – 2002).
72 Interviewed 29 Jun. 2005.
73 Interviewed 29 Jun. 2005.
74 *The Millions* (July/Aug. 1954).
75 *The Millions* (Mar. 1955).
76 *The Millions* (Jan. 1955).
77 *The Millions* (Apr. 1956).
78 *The Millions* (Apr. 1953).
79 *The Millions* (Feb./Mar. 1960).
80 *The Millions* (Apr. 1958).
81 *The Millions* (Oct. 1954).
82 Interviewed 29 June 2005.
83 *The Millions* (Dec. 1958).
84 Bournemouth 1951.
85 *Overseas Bulletin* (May 1954).
86 'Key money' is money given to the landlord in advance for the privilege of renting the premises.
87 *The Millions* (Apr. 1959).
88 Keith Ranger's private diary.
89 Keith Ranger's diary, p. 57.
90 Interviewed 28 June 2005.
91 Services were held in the evening because Friday is the official day of rest in Muslim countries.
92 Personal correspondence.
93 See *Pigtails, Petticoats and the Old School Tie* by Sheila Miller (OMF Books, 1981).

94 Cynthia Goodall, a much-loved teacher who taught at Chefoo School for 10 years, assured me this was so.

95 Personal correspondence.

96 23 June 2005.

97 Interviewed 22 Jun. 2005.

98 By T.C. Hammond (London: Inter-Varsity Fellowship, 1936).

99 Interviewed 25 Jun. 2005.

100 The following description is adapted from Mary's book 'Time to Tell'.

101 *The Millions* (June 1962).

102 *The Bulletin* (Sept. 1959).

103 Interviewed 29 June 2005.

104 Elizabeth Goldsmith, *God Can Be Trusted* (Carlisle: STL, 1996).

105 Interviewed 1 May 2005.

106 Personal correspondence.

107 Dr Moses Tay later became the Anglican Bishop of Singapore and then Archbishop of the South East Province of the Anglican Church. Sadly his wife died just before he became bishop. He then married Cynthia, who trained at the OMF Discipleship Training Centre.

108 Named in commemoration of the time when John Wesley's heart was 'strangely warmed' and his faith took on a new dimension.

109 Interviewed 30 Jun. 2005.

110 Goldsmith, *Get a Grip on Mission* (Nottingham: IVP, 2006).

111 Interviewed 1 Jul. 2005.

Glossary

Chinese languages:

Cantonese – spoken by many people from Guandong province.

Hakka – dialect spoken by the Han Chinese from Guangdong and Fujian, whose ancestors originated in the Henan and Shanxi provinces of northern China.

Hokkien – spoken by many people from Fukien province.

Hing Hwa – minor dialect of Fukien province.

Mandarin – official language of China.

Teocheow – dialect spoken by the Han Chinese who came from a perfecture-level city in Eastern Guangdong.

Other terms

Batu Caves – famous holy site and pilgrimage centre for Hindus north of Kuala Lumpur, housing a temple dedicated to the god Murugan. The main cave is the size of a soccer field.

Datuk – honourific title, equivalent to a knighthood in the UK.

Feast of Hungry Ghosts is celebrated by the Chinese on the 14th night of the seventh lunar month, which is called the Ghost Month. This is the month in which they believe ghosts and spirits come out from the 'lower world' to visit the earth. The feast is the climax of a series in the Ghost Month celebrations. Activities at the feast include preparing ritualistic offering food, and burning hell money to please the visiting ghosts and spirits, as well as deities and ancestors.

Flannelgraph – pictures, usually of Bible stories, with flannel stuck on the back so that they will adhere to a board covered with flannel.

Key money – money demanded up-front when renting a building. May be many times the actual rent.

Lorong – Malay word for a small lane.

Mar Thoma – ancient Indian Church based in Kerala, Southern India. They believe that their roots can be traced right back to the Apostle Thomas.

Orang asli – original tribal peoples of Malaysia.

Thaipusam – annual Hindu festival drawing the largest gathering in Malaysia, nearly one million in AD 2000. It is popularly believed to commemorate the day Lord Siva's consort, the goddess Parvathi, gave her son Murugan a powerful lance to vanquish three demons and their armies.

English-speaking OMF Centres

AUSTRALIA: PO Box 849, Epping, NSW 1710.
Tel: 02-9868-477 e-mail: au@omf.net. www.au.omf.org

CANADA: 5155 Spectrum Way, Building 21, Mississauga, ONT L4W 5A1.
Toll free: 1-888-657-8010. e-mail: omfcanada@omf.ca
www.omf.ca

HONG KONG: PO Box 70505, Kowloon Central PO, Hong Kong. Tel: 852-2398-1823. e-mail: hk@omf.net
www.omf.org.hk

MALAYSIA: 3A Jalan Nipah, off Jalan Ampang, 55000, Kuala Lumpur.
Tel: 603-4257-4263. e-mail: my@omf.net www.omf.org

NEW ZEALAND: PO Box 10159, Dominion Road, Balmoral, Auckland 1030. Tel: 09-630-5778.
e-mail: omfnz@omf.net www.nz.omf.org

PHILIPPINES: QCCPO Box 1997-1159, 1100 Quezon City, M.M. Tel: 632-951-0782. email: ph-hc@omf.net www.omf.org

SINGAPORE: 2 Cluny Road, Singapore 259570. Tel: 65-6475-4592. e-mail: sno@omf.net www.sg.omf.org

UK: Station Approach, Borough Green, Sevenoaks, Kent, TN15 8BG. Tel: 01732-887299. e-mail: omf@omf.org.uk www.omf.org.uk

USA: 10 West Dry Creek Circle, Littleton, CO 80120-4413. Toll Free: 1-800-422-5330. e-mail: omfus@omf.org www.us.omf.org

OMF INTERNATIONAL HEADQUARTERS: 2 Cluny Road, Singapore 259570. Tel: 65-6319-4550. e-mail: ihq@omf.net www.omf.org